the LION in WINTER

JAMES

GOLDMAN

RANDOM HOUSE

the LION
in WINTER

NEW YORK

Second Printing
©Copyright, 1966, by James Goldman
©Copyright, as an unpublished work, 1964, by James Goldman

All rights including the right of reproduction in whole or in part, in any form, are reserved under International and Pan-American Copyright Conventions. Published in New York by Random House, Inc., and simultaneously in Toronto, Canada, by Random House of Canada Limited.

CAUTION: Professionals and amateurs are hereby warned that THE LION IN WINTER, being fully protected under the Copyright Laws of the United States of America, the British Commonwealth, including the Dominion of Canada, and all other countries of the Berne and Universal Copyright Conventions, is subject to royalty. All rights, including professional, amateur, motion picture, recitation, lecturing, public reading, radio and television broadcasting, and the rights of translation into foreign languages, are strictly reserved. Particular emphasis is laid on the question of readings, permission for which must be secured in writing from the author's agent. All inquiries, Monica McCall Inc., 667 Madison Avenue, New York, N.Y. 10021.

Photographs by courtesy of Freidman-Abeles

Library of Congress Catalog Card Number: 66-22253

Manufactured in the United States of America

For *BILL*

The historical material on Henry's reign is considerable insofar as battles, plots, wars, treaties and alliances are concerned. This play, while simplifying the political maneuvering—and combining a meeting of the French and English Kings in 1183 with a Royal Court held at Windsor the following year into a Christmas Court that never was—is based on the available data.

The facts we have, while clear enough as to the outcome of relationships—such things as who kills whom and when—say little if anything about the quality and content of those relationships. The people in this play, their characters and passions, while consistent with the facts we have, are fictions.

There were no laws of primogeniture in Henry's time. It was a rare thing when the King was followed by his eldest son. When kings died, it was open season on the English throne, a fact responsible for much that Henry did.

THE LION IN WINTER *was first presented by Eugene V. Wolsk, Walter A. Hyman and Alan King with Emanuel Azenberg at the Ambassador Theatre in New York City on March 3, 1966, with the following cast:*

(In order of appearance)

HENRY II, King of England	Robert Preston
ALAIS CAPET	Suzanne Grossmann
JOHN	Bruce Scott
GEOFFREY	Dennis Cooney
RICHARD	James Rado
ELEANOR OF AQUITAINE	Rosemary Harris
PHILIP CAPET, King of France	Christopher Walken

Directed by Noel Willman

Scenery and costumes by Will Steven Armstrong

Lighting by Tharon Musser

Incidental music by Thomas Wagner

Production Manager: Jose Vega

The Time: Christmas, 1183.
The Place: Henry's palace at Chinon, France.
The Set: The palace at Chinon was famous for its grace and beauty. The arches, walls and columns of the set, though stone, are soft and light. There are no signs of royal wealth or pomp. The rooms in which the play occurs are simple, airy, clean and as free of furniture and things as possible.

The LION in WINTER

ACT ONE

ALAIS's *chamber. It is a small and graceful room, containing just a bench, a chest and a chair. Late afternoon light streams in through a window.*

As the curtain rises, ALAIS CAPET, *dressed for a state occasion, is removing a small crown from her exquisite head. She is twenty-three, serenely beautiful, and though glaring at him at the moment, unmistakably in love with* HENRY PLANTAGENET. *He has just turned fifty, an age at which, in his time, men were either old or dead. Not* HENRY. *Though arthritis comes occasionally and new battle wounds don't heal the way the old ones did, he still is very nearly all he ever was. He is enjoying that final rush of physical and mental vigor that comes to some men not before the end but just before the start of the decline. He wears, as always, plain and unimpressive clothes.*

As ALAIS *takes off her crown,* HENRY *turns to her and, with the beginnings of impatience, speaks.*

HENRY You must know that's a futile gesture. Come along.

ALAIS No; I'll stay here and you can send reports.

HENRY It's going to be a jungle of a day: if I start growling now, I'll never last.

3

ALAIS   You'll last. You're like the rocks at Stonehenge; nothing knocks you down.

HENRY   In these rooms, Alais, on this Christmas, I have all the enemies I need.

ALAIS   You have more than you think.

HENRY   Are you one? Has my willow turned to poison oak?

ALAIS   If I decided to be trouble, Henry, how much trouble could I be?

HENRY   Not much. You don't matter to the others; only me.

ALAIS   How great a matter am I?

HENRY   Alais, in my time I've known contessas, milk-maids, courtesans and novices, whores, gypsies, jades and little boys, but nowhere in God's Western world have I found anyone to love but you.

ALAIS   And Rosamund.

HENRY   She's dead.

ALAIS   And Eleanor.

HENRY   The new Medusa? My good wife?

ALAIS   How is your Queen?

HENRY   Decaying, I suppose.

ALAIS   You haven't seen her?

HENRY   No, nor smelled nor touched nor tasted. Don't be jealous of the gorgon; she is not among the things I love.

4

How many husbands do you know who dungeon up their wives? I haven't kept the great bitch in the keep for ten years out of passionate attachment. Come. I've heard she's aging badly; let's go look.

ALAIS   Would it be troublesome if I betrayed you?

HENRY   We've no secrets, Eleanor and I. How can you possibly betray me?

ALAIS   I could give away your plans.

HENRY   You don't know what they are.

ALAIS   I know you want to disinherit Richard.

HENRY   So does Eleanor. She knows young Henry's dead. The Young King died in summer and I haven't named an heir. She knows I want John on the throne and I know she wants Richard. We are very frank about it.

ALAIS   Henry, I can't be your mistress if I'm married to your son.

HENRY   Why can't you? Johnny wouldn't mind.

ALAIS   I do not like your Johnny.

HENRY   He's a good boy.

ALAIS   He's got pimples and he smells of compost.

HENRY   He's just sixteen; he can't help the pimples.

ALAIS   He could bathe.

HENRY   It isn't such a dreadful thing to be a Queen of England. Not all eyes will weep for you.

ALAIS   Will yours?

HENRY   I don't know. Very likely.

ALAIS   All I want is not to lose you. Can't you hide me?
Can't I simply disappear?

HENRY   You know you can't. Your little brother Philip's
King of France now and he wants your wedding or your
dowry back. I only took you for your dowry. You were
seven. Two big knees and two big eyes and that's all.
How was I to know?

ALAIS   Let Philip have the dowry back. It isn't much.

HENRY   I can't. The Vexin is a little county but it's vital
to me.

ALAIS   And I'm not.

HENRY   It's been my luck to fall in love with landed
women. When I married Eleanor, I thought: "You lucky
man. The richest woman in the world. She owns the
Aquitaine, the greatest province on the Continent—and
beautiful as well." She was, you know.

ALAIS   And you adored her.

HENRY   Memory fails. There may have been an era when
I did. (*Arranging a wisp of her hair*) Let's have one
strand askew; nothing in life has any business being
perfect.

ALAIS   Henry, I was brought up to be dutiful. I smile a
lot, bend easily and hope for very little. It is useful train-
ing and it's made a lot of hard things possible. But,
Henry, not this thing.

HENRY   I've had them summoned and I'll have you by
me. With the headdress or without it.

ALAIS   Oh, what difference does it make who's king?

HENRY   What difference?

ALAIS   Have you found religion, Henry? Are you going to look down from the clouds and see who's sitting in your place?

HENRY   I've got to know before I die. I've built an empire and I've got to know it's going to last. I've put together England and I've added to it half of France. I am the greatest power in a thousand years. And after me comes John. If I can't leave this state to John, I've lived for nothing.

ALAIS   John doesn't care for you at all.

HENRY   We love each other deeply.

ALAIS   None of them has any love for you.

HENRY   Because we fight? Tell me they all three want the crown, I'll tell you it's a feeble prince that doesn't. They may snap at me or plot and that makes them the kind of sons I want. I've snapped and plotted all my life: there is no other way to be a king, alive and fifty all at once.

ALAIS   I'm going to fight for you.

HENRY   Oh, fine.

ALAIS   When I was sixteen and we started this depraved relationship, I left everything to you. I lap sat, drank my milk and did what I was told. Not any more. Your cherub's twenty-three now and she's going to fight.

HENRY   With mace and chain?

ALAIS   With anything that I can think of.

7

HENRY That's exactly what I need: another mind at work. Try; you can hear the thinking through the walls. There's Geoffrey, humming treachery. And Richard, growling out for gore. And Eleanor, she's thinking heavy thoughts like molten lead and marble slabs. My house is full of intellectual activity.

ALAIS Add mine.

HENRY Alais, Alais—I don't plan to give you up. I don't plan to give up anything. I'll make alliances and bargains, threaten, beg, break heads and hearts, and when I'm done, I'll make an heir of John, a petty prince of Richard and I'll still have you.

ALAIS When can I believe you, Henry?

HENRY Always; even when I lie.

ALAIS How much is it safe to hope for?

HENRY Everything.

ALAIS But with so many enemies—

HENRY I know—and some of them are smarter folk than I or crueler or more ruthless or dishonest. But not all rolled in one. The priests write all the history these days and they'll do me justice. Henry, they'll say, was a master bastard. (*Extending his arm*) Come; let's go downstairs and meet the family.
(*She moves to join him*)

Dim and blackout

SCENE 2

A Reception Hall, immediately following. It is a bright and spacious room. There is a bench, a large refectory table and a massive chair. A pile of holly boughs lies stacked in a corner.

*The young Plantagenets—*RICHARD, GEOFFREY *and* JOHN *—are entering as the lights rise.*

RICHARD LIONHEART, *at twenty-six, looks like his legend. He is handsome, graceful and impressive. He has been a famous soldier since his middle teens, and justly so; war is his profession and he is good at it.*

GEOFFREY, *Count of Brittany, is twenty-five. A man of energy and verve, he is attractive, charming and the owner of the best brain of a brainy family.*

JOHN, *at sixteen, does indeed have pimples. He is a charming-looking boy in spite of them, sweet-faced and totally adorable.*

They are bowing each other into the room when we see them.

JOHN After you.

GEOFFREY No; after you.

9

RICHARD   No; after you.

JOHN (*Delighted with himself as he skips into the room*)
Oh, have it your way; after me.

RICHARD (*Following in, along with* GEOFFREY) You do
keep growing, Johnny.

JOHN (*Agreeing cheerfully*) Every way but up. Look:
holly. (*Beginning to hang the holly boughs*) I love
Christmas.

GEOFFREY   Warm and rosy time. The hot wine steams,
the Yule log roars and we're the fat that's in the fire.
She's here, you know.

JOHN   Who?

RICHARD   Mother.

GEOFFREY   Since this morning.

RICHARD   Have you seen her?

GEOFFREY   Haven't you?

RICHARD   We're not as friendly as we were.

GEOFFREY   Does she still favor you?

RICHARD   Does she or doesn't she?

JOHN   If I'm supposed to make a fuss and kiss her hairy
cheek, I won't.

RICHARD   What you kiss, little prince, is up to you.

JOHN   I'm Father's favorite; that's what counts.

RICHARD   You hardly know me, Johnny, so I beg you to

believe my reputation: I'm a constant soldier and a sometime poet and I will be king.

JOHN Just you remember: Father loves me best.

ELEANOR (*Sweeping in*) The way you bicker it's a wonder that he cares for any of you.
> (ELEANOR OF AQUITAINE *is sixty-one and looks nothing like it. She is a truly handsome woman of great temperament, authority and presence. She has been a queen of international importance for forty-six years and you know it. Finally, she is that most unusual thing: a genuinely feminine woman thoroughly capable of holding her own in a man's world*)

GEOFFREY Mother.

ELEANOR Geoffrey—but I do have handsome children. John—you're so clean and neat. Henry takes good care of you. And Richard. Don't look sullen, dear; it makes your eyes go small and piggy and your chin look weak. Where's Henry?

RICHARD Upstairs with the family whore.

ELEANOR That is a mean and tawdry way to talk about your fiancée.

JOHN My fiancée.

ELEANOR Whosever fiancée, I brought her up and she is dear to me and gentle. Have we seen the French King yet?

GEOFFREY Not yet.

ELEANOR Let's hope he's grown up like his father—simon pure and simon simple. Good, good Louis; if I'd managed sons for him instead of all those little girls, I'd still be stuck with being Queen of France and we should not have known each other. Such, my angels, is the role of sex in history. How's your father?

JOHN Do you care?

ELEANOR More deeply, lamb, than you can possibly imagine. Is my hair in place? I've given up the looking glass; quicksilver has no sense of tact.

RICHARD He still plans to make John king.

ELEANOR Of course he does. My, what a greedy little trinity you are: king, king, king. Two of you must learn to live with disappointment.

HENRY (*Entering, with* ALAIS) Ah—but which two?

ELEANOR Let's deny them all and live forever.

HENRY Tusk to tusk through all eternity. How was your crossing? Did the Channel part for you?

ELEANOR It went flat when I told it to; I didn't think to ask for more. How dear of you to let me out of jail.

HENRY It's only for the holidays.

ELEANOR Like school. You keep me young. Here's gentle Alais. (*As* ALAIS *starts to curtsy*) No, no; greet me like you used to. (*Hugging her*) Fragile I am not: affection is a pressure I can bear.

HENRY I've had the French King sent for. We will have a tactile conversation, like two surgeons looking for a lump. We'll state positions and I'll make the first of many offers. He'll refuse it, naturally, I'll make a better one and so on through the holidays until I win. For the duration of this joyous ritual, you will give, to your father, your support.

RICHARD Why will I?

ELEANOR Out of duty, dear. (*To* HENRY) Tell me, what's Philip like? I hear he's quite impressive for a boy of seventeen—

HENRY (*As* PHILIP *enters*) My Lord.

ELEANOR Oh—and you are. I'm Eleanor, who might have been your mother. All the others here you know.

PHILIP (PHILIP CAPET *is indeed impressive. He is tall, well-proportioned and handsome without being at all pretty. His manner is open, direct and simple and he smiles easily. He has been King of France for three years and has learned a great deal. He bows*) Queen Eleanor—Your Grace.

HENRY My Lord. Welcome to Chinon.

PHILIP Sir.

HENRY Your grievances, as we have understood them, have to do with Princess Alais and her dowry.

PHILIP Sixteen years ago you made a treaty with us. It is time its terms were executed.

HENRY We are willing to discuss it.

PHILIP Our position comes to this: that you will either hold the marriage or return the Vexin. Alais marries Richard or we'll have the county back at once.

HENRY That's clear, concise and well presented. My position is— Well, frankly, Philip, it's a tangle. Once I'm dead, who's to be king? I could draw papers till my scribes drop or the ink runs out and once I died, unless I've left behind me three contented sons, my lands will split three ways in civil war. You see my problem?

PHILIP   Clearly; but it's yours, not mine.

HENRY   Two years ago the Queen and I, for reasons passing understanding, gave the Aquitaine to Richard. That makes Richard very powerful. How can I give him Alais, too? The man she marries has you for an ally.

PHILIP   It's their wedding or the Vexin back. Those are the terms you made with Louis.

HENRY   True but academic, lad. The Vexin's mine.

PHILIP   By what authority?

HENRY   It's got my troops all over it: that makes it mine. Now hear me, boy. You take what memories you have of me and mark them out of date. I'm not your father's friend, now; I'm his son's opponent.

PHILIP   I'm a king: I'm no man's boy.

HENRY   A king? Because you put your ass on purple cushions?

PHILIP   Sir.
        (*He turns on his heel and starts to go*)

HENRY   Philip, you haven't got the feel of this at all. Use all your voices: when I bellow, bellow back.

PHILIP   I'll mark that down.

HENRY   This, too. We are the world in small. A nation is a human thing; it does what we do, for our reasons.

Surely, if we're civilized, it must be possible to put the knives away. We can make peace. We have it in our hands.

PHILIP I've tutors of my own. Will that be all?

HENRY Oh, think. You came here for a reason. You've made demands of me. Now don't you want to ask me if I've got an offer?

PHILIP Have you got an offer?

HENRY Not yet—but I'll think of one. (PHILIP *starts off again*) Oh, by the way . . . (*At the doorway,* PHILIP *turns*) You're better at this than I thought you'd be.

PHILIP (*Smiling*) I wasn't sure you'd noticed.
    (*He exits*)

HENRY Well—what shall we hang? The holly or each other?

ELEANOR You can't read your sons at all. That isn't anger they're projecting; it's anxiety.

HENRY I read them. I know Richard's moods and Johnny's faces and the thought behind the pitch of Geoffrey's voice. The trouble's at the other end; they don't know me. (*Turning to his sons*) There is a legend of a king called Lear with whom I have a lot in common. Both of us have kingdoms and three children we adore and both of us are old. But there it stops. He cut his kingdom into bits. I can't do that. I've built this house and it will stand. What I have architected, you will not destroy.

RICHARD Would you say, Father, that I have the makings of a king?

HENRY A splendid king.

RICHARD Would you expect me, Father, to be disinherited without a fight?

HENRY Of course you'll fight. I raised you to.

RICHARD I don't care what you offer Philip. I don't care what plans you make. I'll have the Aquitaine and Alais and the crown. I'll have them all.

JOHN You're going to love my coronation.

RICHARD I won't give up one to get the other. I won't trade off Alais or the Aquitaine to this (*Indicating* JOHN) —this walking pustule. No, your loving son will not.
(*He exits*)

JOHN Did you hear what he called me?

ELEANOR Clearly, dear. Now run along; it's nearly dinner-time.

JOHN I only do what Father tells me.

HENRY Go and eat.

JOHN Did I say something wrong? I'm always saying something wrong. All right, I'll eat, I'll eat.
(*He exits*)

ELEANOR And that's to be the king.

GEOFFREY And I'm to be his chancellor. Has he told you? John will rule the country while I run it. That's to say, he gets to spend the taxes that I get to raise.

ELEANOR How nice for you.

GEOFFREY It's not as nice as being king.

HENRY We've made you Duke of Brittany. Is that so little?

GEOFFREY No one ever thinks of crowns and mentions Geoff. Why is that? I make out three prizes here—a throne, a princess and the Aquitaine. Three prizes and three sons; but no one ever says, "Here, Geoff, here Geoff boy, here's a bone for you."

HENRY I should have thought that being chancellor was a satisfying bone.

GEOFFREY It isn't power that I feel deprived of; it's the mention that I miss. There's no affection for me here. You wouldn't think I'd want that, would you?
    (*He exits*)

ELEANOR Henry, I have a confession.

HENRY Yes?

ELEANOR I don't much like our children. (*To* ALAIS) Only you—the child I raised but didn't bear.

ALAIS You never cared for me.

ELEANOR I did and do. Believe me, Henry's bed is Henry's province: he can people it with sheep for all I care. Which, on occasion, he has done.

HENRY Still that? When Rosamund's been dead for seven years?

ELEANOR Two months and eighteen days. I never liked her much.

HENRY You count the days?

ELEANOR I made the numbers up. (*To* ALAIS) He found Miss Clifford in the mists of Wales and brought her home for closer observation. Liking what he saw, he scrutinized her many years. He loved her deeply and she him. And yet, my dear, when Henry had to choose between his lady and my lands—

ALAIS He'll leave me if he has to; I know that.

ELEANOR Poor Alais.

ALAIS There's no sport in hurting me; it is so easy.

ELEANOR After all the years of love, the hair I've brushed and braided and the tears I've kissed away, do you think I could bring myself to hurt you?

ALAIS Eleanor, with both hands tied behind you. (*She exits*)

HENRY She is lovely, isn't she?

ELEANOR Yes, very.

HENRY If I'd chosen, who could I have picked to love to gall you more?

ELEANOR There's no one. (*Moving to the holly boughs*) Come on; let's finish Christmasing the place.

HENRY Time hasn't done a thing but wrinkle you.

ELEANOR It hasn't even done that. I have borne six girls, five boys and thirty-one connubial years of you. How am I possible?

HENRY (*Joining her in hanging holly*) There are moments when I miss you.

ELEANOR Many?

HENRY Do you doubt it?

ELEANOR (*Rumpling his hair*) That's my woolly sheep dog. So wee Johnny gets the crown.

HENRY I've heard it rumored but I don't believe it.

ELEANOR Losing Alais will be hard, for you do love her.

HENRY It's an old man's last attachment; nothing more. How hard do you find living in your castle?

ELEANOR It was difficult in the beginning but that's past. I find I've seen the world enough. I have my maids and menials in my courtyard and I hold my little court. It suits me now.

HENRY I'll never let you loose. You led too many civil wars against me.

ELEANOR And I damn near won the last one. Still, as long as I get trotted out for Christmas Courts and state occasions now and then—for I do like to see you—it's enough. Do you still need the Vexin, Henry?

HENRY Need you ask?

ELEANOR My strategy is ten years old.

HENRY It is as crucial as it ever was. My troops there are a day away from Paris, just a march of twenty miles. I must keep it.

ELEANOR (*Surveying the holly*) - I'd say that's all the jollying this room can stand. I'm famished. Let's go in to dinner.

HENRY (*Extending his arm*) Arm in arm.

ELEANOR (*Taking his arm and smiling at him*)   And hand in hand. You're still a marvel of a man.

HENRY   And you're my lady.

ELEANOR   Henry, dear, if Alais doesn't marry Richard, I will see you lose the Vexin.

HENRY   Well, I thought you'd never say it.

ELEANOR   I can do it.

HENRY   You can try.

ELEANOR   My Richard is the next king, not your John. I know you, Henry. I know every twist and bend you've got and I'll be waiting round each corner for you.

HENRY   Do you truly care who's king?

ELEANOR   I care because you care so much.

HENRY   I might surprise you. Eleanor, I've fought and bargained all these years as if the only thing I lived for was what happened after I was dead. I've something else to live for now. I've blundered onto peace.

ELEANOR   On Christmas Eve.

HENRY   Since Louis died, while Philip grew, I've had no France to fight. And in that lull, I've found how good it is to write a law or make a tax more fair or sit in judgment to decide which peasant gets a cow. There is, I tell you, nothing more important in the world. And now the French boy's big enough and I am sick of war.

ELEANOR   Come to your question, Henry; make the plea. What would you have me do? Give out, give up, give in?

HENRY   Give me a little peace.

ELEANOR   A little? Why so modest? How about eternal peace? Now there's a thought.

HENRY   If you oppose me, I will strike you any way I can.

ELEANOR   Of course you will.

HENRY (*Taking her arm as before*)   We have a hundred barons we should look the loving couple for.

ELEANOR (*Smiling at him*)   Can you read love in that?

HENRY   And permanent affection.

ELEANOR (*As they start, grand and stately, for the wings*) Henry?

HENRY   Madam?

ELEANOR   Did you ever love me?

HENRY   No.

ELEANOR   Good. That will make this pleasanter.

Dim and blackout

ELEANOR's *chamber, some time later. A plain and pleas-
ant room, it holds a chair, a table and a low wood chest.
Soft tapestries give warmth and color. As the lights rise,*
ELEANOR *is seated at the table wrapping Christmas presents.
She looks up as* RICHARD *appears.*

RICHARD   All right. I've come. I'm here. What was it you
wanted?

ELEANOR   Just to talk. We haven't been alone, the two of
us, in— How long is it, lamb? Two years? You look fit.
War agrees with you. I keep informed. I follow all your
slaughters from a distance. Do sit down.

RICHARD   Is this an audience, a goodnight kiss with cook-
ies or an ambush?

ELEANOR   Let us hope it's a reunion. Must you look so
stern? I sent for you to say I want your love again but
I can't say it to a face like that.

RICHARD   My love, of all things. What could you want it
for?

ELEANOR   Why, for itself. What other purpose could I
have?

RICHARD You'll tell me when you're ready to.

ELEANOR I scheme a lot; I know. I plot and plan. That's how a queen in prison spends her time. But there is more to me than that. My mind's not disembodied. Can't I say I love a son and be believed?

RICHARD If I were you, I'd try another tack. I have no dammed-up floods of passion for you. There's no chance I'll overflow.

ELEANOR You are a dull boy.

RICHARD Am I?

ELEANOR Dull as plainsong: la, la, la, forever on one note. I gave the Church up out of boredom. I can do as much for you.

RICHARD You'll never give me up; not while I hold the Aquitaine.

ELEANOR You think I'm motivated by a love of real estate?

RICHARD I think you want it back. You're so deceitful you can't ask for water when you're thirsty. We could tangle spiders in the webs you weave.

ELEANOR If I'm so devious, why don't you go? Don't stand there quivering in limbo. Love me, little lamb, or leave me.

RICHARD (*Not moving*) Leave you, madam? With pure joy.

ELEANOR Departure is a simple act. You put the left foot down and then the right.

JOHN (*Entering, in high spirits, followed by* GEOFFREY) Mother—

ELEANOR Hush, dear. Mother's fighting.

JOHN Father's coming with the treaty terms.

ELEANOR No doubt he's told you what they are.

JOHN He doesn't have to. Don't you think I know which end is up?

ELEANOR Of course you do, dear. Has he put the terms to Philip?

HENRY (*Entering, with* ALAIS) Not yet, but we're shortly granting him an audience. I hope you'll all attend.

ELEANOR Are we to know the terms or have you come to tease us?

HENRY Not at all. The terms are these.

RICHARD What are you giving up to Philip? What of mine?

JOHN Whatever you've got goes to me.

GEOFFREY And what's the nothing Geoffrey gets?

HENRY For God's sake, boys, you can't all three be king.

RICHARD All three of us can try.

HENRY That's pointless now. The treaty calls for you to marry Alais and you shall. I want you to succeed me, Richard. Alais and the crown: I give you both.

RICHARD I've got no sense of humor. If I did, I'd laugh.

HENRY I've used you badly, haven't I?

RICHARD You've used me cleverly and well.

HENRY Not any more. I mean to do it.

JOHN What about me? I'm your favorite, I'm the one you love.

HENRY John, I can't help myself. Stand next to Richard. See how you compare. Could you keep anything I gave you? Could you beat him on the field?

JOHN You could.

HENRY But, John, I won't be there.

JOHN Let's fight him now.

HENRY How can I? There's no way to win. I'm losing too, John. All my dreams for you are lost.

JOHN You've led me on.

HENRY I never meant to.

JOHN You're a failure as a father, you know that.

HENRY I'm sorry, John.

JOHN Not yet you're not. But I'll do something terrible and you'll be sorry then.

ELEANOR Did you rehearse all this or are you improvising?

HENRY Good God, woman, face the facts.

ELEANOR Which ones? We've got so many.

HENRY Power is the only fact. (*Indicating* RICHARD) He is our ablest son. He is the strongest, isn't he? How can

I keep him from the crown? He'd only take it if I didn't give it to him.

RICHARD No—you'd make me fight to get it. I know you: you'd never give me everything.

HENRY True—and I haven't. You get Alais and you get the kingdom but I get the one thing I want most. If you're king, England stays intact. I get that. It's all yours now—the girl, the crown, the whole black bloody business. Isn't that enough?
(*He exits*)

ALAIS I don't know who's to be congratulated. Not me, certainly. (*To* ELEANOR) You got me for your Richard. How'd you manage it? Did you tell him he's your woolly lamb? Or say how much you like it in your castle?

ELEANOR It's all lies but I told him.

ALAIS Kings, queens, knights everywhere you look and I'm the only pawn. I haven't got a thing to lose: that makes me dangerous.
(*She exits*)

ELEANOR Poor child.

JOHN Poor John—who says poor John? Don't everybody sob at once. My God, if I went up in flames, there's not a living soul who'd pee on me to put the fire out.

RICHARD Let's strike a flint and see.

JOHN He hates me. Why? What should he hate me for? Am I the eldest son? Am I the heir? Am I the hero? What's my crime? Is it some childhood score, some baby

hurt? When I was six and you were sixteen, did I brutal-
ize you? What?

ELEANOR   For whatever I have done to you, forgive me.

JOHN   What could you have done? You were never close
enough.

ELEANOR   When you were little, you were torn from me:
blame Henry.

JOHN   I was torn from you by midwives and I haven't
seen you since.

ELEANOR   Then blame me if it helps.

RICHARD   No, it's the midwives' fault. They threw the
baby out and kept the afterbirth.

JOHN   You're everything a little brother dreams of. You
know that? I used to dream about you all the time.

ELEANOR   Oh, Johnny . . .

JOHN   That's right, Mother; mother me.

ELEANOR   Yes, if you'd let me.

JOHN   Let you? Let you put your arms around me just the
way you never did? (*They are close*) You can do it.
Think I'm Richard. (*She puts her arms around him*)
That's it. That's the way. Now kiss my scabby cheek
and run your fingers through my hair.

ELEANOR   John, John . . .

JOHN   (*Wrenching away*) No—it's all false. You know
what I am? I'm the family nothing. Geoffrey's smart and
Richard's brave and I'm not anything.

ELEANOR You are to me.

JOHN I'll show you, Eleanor. I haven't lost yet. (*Moving to go*) Geoff.

GEOFFREY In a minute.

JOHN What's that?

GEOFFREY Run along. I'm busy now.

JOHN I give the orders. I'm the master. When I call, you come.

GEOFFREY There's news in Chinon, John. That falling sound was you.

JOHN The woods are full of chancellors.

GEOFFREY And the castle's full of kings.

JOHN Oh, you're not really leaving me?

GEOFFREY No; I've already left.

JOHN I don't care. I don't need anybody.
(*He exits*)

GEOFFREY Well, Mummy, here I am.

ELEANOR John's lost a chancellor, has he?

GEOFFREY And you've gained one.

ELEANOR It's a bitter thing your Mummy has to say.

GEOFFREY She doesn't trust me.

ELEANOR You must know Henry isn't through with John.
He'll keep the Vexin till the moon goes blue from cold

and as for Richard's wedding day, we'll see the second coming first; the needlework alone can last for years.

GEOFFREY I know. You know I know. I know you know I know, we know that Henry knows and Henry knows we know it. We're a knowledgeable family. Do you want my services or don't you?

ELEANOR Why are you dropping John?

GEOFFREY Because you're going to win.

ELEANOR I haven't yet.

GEOFFREY You will with me to help you. I can handle John. He'll swallow anything I tell him and I'll take him by the hand and walk him into any trap you set.

ELEANOR You're good, you're first class, Geoff. Did John agree?

GEOFFREY To what?

ELEANOR To making you his chancellor for betraying me?

GEOFFREY I have some principles.

ELEANOR Then how much did you get from Henry?

GEOFFREY Get from Henry?

ELEANOR What's the fee for selling me to him? Or have you found some way of selling everyone to everybody?

GEOFFREY Not yet, Mummy, but I'm working on it. I don't care who's king but you and Henry do. I want to watch the two of you go picnicking on one another.

ELEANOR Yes, it's true; you really mean it.

GEOFFREY Do you blame me?

ELEANOR You've a gift for hating.

GEOFFREY You're the expert; you should know.

ELEANOR You've loved me all these years.

GEOFFREY Well, God forgive me, I've upset the Queen.
Madam, may you rot.

ELEANOR We need you. Help us.

GEOFFREY What? And miss the fun of selling you?

ELEANOR Be Richard's chancellor.

GEOFFREY Rot.
      (*He exits*)

ELEANOR Oh, Geoffrey. Well, that's how deals are made.
We've got him if we want him. I should like some wine.
Why did I have to have such clever children? He will
sell us all, you know; but only if he thinks we think he
won't. Scenes. I can't touch my sons except in scenes.
(RICHARD *gives her a glass of wine*) What's the matter,
Richard?

Beat

Elanor
approaches
Richard

feels out
his mood

RICHARD Nothing.

ELEANOR It's a heavy thing, your nothing. When I write
or send for you or speak or reach, your nothings come.
Like stones.

RICHARD Don't play a scene with me.

ELEANOR I wouldn't if I could.

RICHARD There'd be no profit in it. That's my one advantage over you. You're wiser, shrewder, more experienced. I'm colder; I feel less.

ELEANOR   Why, you don't know yourself at all. I've known who I am some years now. I had, at one time, many appetites. I wanted poetry and power and the young men who create them both. I even wanted Henry, too, in those days. Now I've only one desire left: to see you king.   *Beat*

RICHARD   The only thing you want to see is Father's vitals on a bed of lettuce. You don't care who wins as long as Henry loses. You'd see Philip on the throne. You'd feed us to the Franks or hand us to the Holy Romans. You'd do anything.

ELEANOR   (*Nodding wearily*)   That's good to know.

RICHARD   You are Medea to the teeth but this is one son you won't use for vengeance on your husband.

ELEANOR   I could bend you. I could wear you like a bracelet—but I'd sooner die.

RICHARD   You're old enough to die, in any case.

ELEANOR   How my captivity has changed you. Henry   *— Beat*
meant to hurt me and he's hacked you up instead. More wine. (*He takes the glass and goes to pour. She gazes at the hand that held the glass*) Men coveted this talon once. Henry was eighteen when we met and I was Queen of France. He came down from the North to Paris with a mind like Aristotle's and a form like mortal sin. We shattered the Commandments on the spot. I spent three months annulling Louis and in spring, in May not far from here, we married. Young Count Henry and his Countess. But in three years' time, I was his

Queen and he was King of England. Done at twenty-one. Five years your junior, General.

RICHARD   I can count.

ELEANOR   No doubt the picture of your parents being fond does not hang in your gallery—but we were fond. There was no Thomas Becket then, or Rosamund. No rivals—only me. And then young Henry came and you and all the other blossoms in my garden. Yes, if I'd been sterile, darling, I'd be happier today.

RICHARD   Is that designed to hurt me?

ELEANOR   What a waste. I've fought with Henry over who comes next, whose dawn is it and which son gets the sunset and we'll never live to see it. Look at you. I loved you more than Henry and it's cost me everything.

RICHARD   What do you want?

ELEANOR   I want us back the way we were.

RICHARD   That's not it.

ELEANOR   All right, then. I want the Aquitaine.

RICHARD   Now that's the mother I remember.

ELEANOR   No, it's not at all, but if you find her more congenial, she's the one you'll get. We can win. I can get you Alais. I can make the marriage happen—but I've got to have the Aquitaine to do it. I must have it back.

RICHARD   You were better in your scene with Geoffrey.

ELEANOR   Shall I write my will? "To Richard, everything." Would you believe me then? Where's paper?

32

RICHARD Paper burns.

ELEANOR And tears and turns to pudding in the rain. What can I do?

RICHARD I did think Geoffrey put it nicely. You can rot.

Beat

ELEANOR I love you.

RICHARD You love nothing. You are incomplete. The human parts of you are missing. You're as dead as you are deadly.

ELEANOR Don't leave me.

RICHARD You were lovely once. I've seen the pictures.

ELEANOR Oh, don't you remember how you loved me?

RICHARD Vaguely—like a legend.

ELEANOR You remember. We were always hand in hand. (*Thrusting her hand in his*) That's how it felt.

RICHARD As coarse and hot as that.

ELEANOR (*Snatching her hand away*) This won't burn. I'll scratch a will on this. (*Baring her forearm, with a small knife suddenly in her other hand*) To Richard, everything.

RICHARD (*As she draws the blade across the flesh*) Mother!

Beat

ELEANOR Remember how I taught you numbers and the lute and poetry.

RICHARD (*As they hold each other*) Mother.

33

ELEANOR See? You do remember. I taught you dancing, too, and languages and all the music that I knew and how to love what's beautiful. The sun was warmer then and we were every day together.

Dim and blackout

34

SCENE 4

The Reception Hall, immediately following. A Christmas tree has been added to the room. JOHN *is drinking from a bottle as the lights rise.* GEOFFREY *enters, calling.*

GEOFFREY John—there you are.

JOHN Go find yourself another fool.

GEOFFREY You're angry: good. Now, here's my plan.

JOHN You are a rancid bastard. Want to fight?

GEOFFREY John, use your head. Would I betray you?

JOHN Why not? Everybody else does.

GEOFFREY John, I only turned on you to get their confidence. It worked; they trust me.

JOHN I tell you, your leg could fall off at the pelvis and I wouldn't trust the stump to bleed.

GEOFFREY If you're not king, I'm nothing. You're my way to power, John.

JOHN I still don't trust you.

GEOFFREY Always put your faith in vices. Trust my sly-

35

ness if you think I'm sly. Make use of me, deceive me, cast me off—but not until I've made you king.

JOHN You think I can't out-think you, do you? All right, what's your plan?

GEOFFREY We've got to make a deal with Philip.

JOHN Why?

GEOFFREY Because you're out and Richard's in.

JOHN What kind of deal?

GEOFFREY A war. If we three join and fight now, we can finish Richard off.

JOHN You mean destroy him?

GEOFFREY Yes.

JOHN And Mother, too?

GEOFFREY And Mother, too. Well, do we do it? Is it on?

JOHN I've got to think.

GEOFFREY We're extra princes now. You know where extra princes go.

JOHN Down?

GEOFFREY Very down.

PHILIP (Entering) I see I'm early for my audience. Or am I late?

GEOFFREY No, you're exquisitely on time. I feel the strangest sense of kinship with you, Philip.

PHILIP So you've sensed it, too.

GEOFFREY How far around the corner were you?

PHILIP How'd you know?

GEOFFREY You came in so conveniently.

PHILIP I'll learn.

GEOFFREY Well, was there anything you didn't overhear?

PHILIP John's answer. Does he want a war or doesn't he?

GEOFFREY Do you? If John asks for your soldiers, will he get them?

PHILIP If John wants a war, he's got one.

GEOFFREY John, you hear that?

JOHN I'm still thinking.

GEOFFREY Let me help. It's either Richard on the throne or you.

JOHN (*To* PHILIP) You think we'd win?

PHILIP I know it.

JOHN Father's coming.

GEOFFREY (*Moving to exit*) This way. We've got plans to make. (*Turning back as* PHILIP *exits*) John.

JOHN In a minute.
(GEOFFREY *exits*)

HENRY (*Entering with* ALAIS. *To* ALAIS) I'd appreciate a little quiet confidence. I have enough nits picking at me.

JOHN Father, have you got a minute?

HENRY What for?

JOHN   If you had a minute, we could talk.

HENRY   I'm busy now. Have you seen Philip?

JOHN   Look: you know that hunting trip we're taking on my birthday?

HENRY   Well?

JOHN   Forget it. I'm not going.

HENRY   Why not?

JOHN   I'm just not.

HENRY   But, John, the trip's all planned.

JOHN   *(Moving to go)*   I'll go get Philip for you.

HENRY   You did have a good time last year, didn't you?

JOHN   I loved it.

HENRY   What's wrong, lad?

JOHN   You're busy.

HENRY   True enough but—

JOHN   You've got more important things to do.

HENRY   I can't make things all right if I don't know what's wrong.

JOHN   You're giving Richard everything.

HENRY   You think I'd do that?

JOHN   You don't love me any more.

HENRY   Don't pout—and stand up straight. How often do I have to tell you?

Robert Preston, as HENRY II, argues with Christopher Walken, who plays PHILIP CAPET, King of France. Watching are Bruce Scott and Rosemary Harris, as JOHN and ELEANOR OF AQUITAINE.

JOHN   When's my coronation?

HENRY   When I say so.

JOHN   That's no answer.
(*He starts off*)

HENRY   John.

JOHN   Tell her how much you love her. You're a wonder with the women.
(*He exits*)

HENRY   What in hell was that about?

ALAIS   He heard you disinherit him upstairs and wondered if you meant it.

HENRY   If I meant it? When I've fathered him and mothered him and babied him? He's all I've got. How often does he have to hear it? Every supper? Should we start the soup with who we love and who we don't?

ALAIS   I heard you promise me to Richard.

HENRY   You don't think I meant it?

ALAIS   I think you enjoy it, passing me from hand to hand. What am I to you—a collection plate? Or am I all you've got, like John?

HENRY   I've got to get the Aquitaine for John.

ALAIS   I talk people and you answer back in provinces.

HENRY   They get mixed up. What's the Aquitaine to Eleanor? It's not a province, it's a way to torture me. That's why she's upstairs wooing Richard, wheezing on the coals. She'll squeeze it out of him. God, but I'd love to eavesdrop. (*Doing* ELEANOR) I taught you prancing, lamb, and lute and flute—

ELEANOR (*Entering, carrying a great pile of Christmas boxes*) That's marvelous; it's absolutely me. (*He takes some from her*) There you are. I thought as long as I was coming down I'd bring them. Where's the tree?

HENRY (*Leading the way to it*) Whatever are you giving me?

ELEANOR You're such a child: you always ask.

HENRY (*Reading from a package*) To Henry. (*Weighing it*) Heavy. (*Delighted*) It's my headstone. Eleanor, you spoil me.

ELEANOR I never could deny you anything.

ALAIS You've grown old gracefully, you two; I'll give you that.

HENRY (*As* ALAIS *starts to go*) Don't go. It nettles her to see how much I need you.

ALAIS You need me, Henry, like a tailor needs a tinker's dam.

HENRY Alais—

ALAIS I know that look. He's going to say he loves me.

HENRY Like my life. (*She turns sharply and exits*) I talk like that to keep her spirits up. Well, how'd you do with Richard? Did you break his heart?

ELEANOR You think he ought to give me back the Aquitaine?

HENRY I can't think why he shouldn't. After all, I've promised him the throne.

ELEANOR The boy keeps wondering if your promises are any good.

HENRY There's no sense asking if the air's good when there's nothing else to breathe.

ELEANOR Exactly what I told him.

HENRY Have you got it? Will he give it back?

ELEANOR How can you think I'd ever pass it on to John?

HENRY It matters to me desperately.

ELEANOR Why should it? Does it matter what comes after us?

HENRY Ask any sculptor, ask Praxiteles, "Why don't you work in butter?" Eleanor, because it doesn't last.

ELEANOR Is Johnny bronze? He'll go as green from mold as any of our sons.

HENRY I know that. Richard gets the throne. You heard my promise. What else do you want?

ELEANOR No Aquitaine for John.

HENRY I've got to give him something. Isn't some agreement possible?

ELEANOR Love, in a world where carpenters get resurrected, anything is possible.

HENRY You bore him, dammit; he's your son.

ELEANOR Oh, heavens yes. Two hundred eighty days I

bore him. I recall them all. You'd only just found Rosamund.

HENRY   Why her so damn particularly? I've found other
women.

ELEANOR   Countless others.

HENRY   What's your count? Let's have a tally of the bed-
spreads you've spread out on.

ELEANOR   Thomas Becket's.

HENRY   That's a lie.

ELEANOR   I know it. Jealousy looks silly on us, Henry.

HENRY   Doesn't it.

ELEANOR   You still care what I do.

HENRY   I want the Aquitaine for John. I want it and I'll
have it.

ELEANOR   Is that menace you're conveying? Is it to be torture? Will you boil me or stretch me, which? Or am I
to be perforated?

HENRY   I have the documents and you will sign.

ELEANOR   How can you force me to? Threats? Sign or I
refuse to feed you? Tears? Oh, sign before my heart goes
crack. Bribes, offers, deals? I'm like the earth, old man;
there isn't any way around me.

HENRY   I adore you.

ELEANOR   Save your aching arches; that road is closed.

HENRY   I've got an offer for you, *ma jolie.*

ELEANOR A deal, a deal. I give the richest province on the Continent to John for what? You tell me, mastermind. For what?

HENRY Your freedom.

ELEANOR Oh.

HENRY Once Johnny has the Aquitaine, you're free. I'll let you out. Think: on the loose in London, winters in Provence, impromptu trips to visit Richard anywhere he's killing people. All that for a signature.

ELEANOR You're good.

HENRY I thought it might appeal to you. You always fancied traveling.

ELEANOR Yes, I did. I even made poor Louis take me on Crusade. How's that for blasphemy? I dressed my maids as Amazons and rode bare-breasted halfway to Damascus. Louis had a seizure and I damn near died of windburn but the troops were dazzled. Henry, I'm against the wall.

HENRY Because I've put you there, don't think I like to see it.

ELEANOR I believe it; you do feel for me. To be a prisoner, to be bricked in when you've known the world—I'll never know how I've survived. These ten years, Henry, have been unimaginable. And you can offer me the only thing I want if I give up the only thing I treasure and still feel for me. You give your falcons more affection than I get.

HENRY My falcons treat me better.

ELEANOR Handle me with iron gloves, then.

HENRY Sign the papers and we'll break the happy news. The Queen is free, John joins the landed gentry, Philip's satisfied and Richard gets a princess.

ELEANOR Yes. Let's have it done. I'll sign. On one condition.

HENRY Name it.

ELEANOR Have the wedding now.

HENRY What's that?

ELEANOR Why, I've surprised you. Surely it's not sudden. They've been marching down the aisle for sixteen years and that's a long walk. John can be the best man—that's a laugh—and you can give the bride away. I want to watch you do it.

HENRY Alais—I can live without her.

ELEANOR And I thought you loved her.

HENRY So I do.

ELEANOR Thank God. You frightened me: I was afraid this wouldn't hurt.

HENRY You fill me full of fear and pity. What a tragedy you are.

ELEANOR I wonder, do you ever wonder if I slept with Geoffrey?

HENRY With my father?

ELEANOR It's not true but one hears rumors. Don't you ever wonder?

HENRY Is it rich, despising me? Is it rewarding?

ELEANOR No—it's terrible.

HENRY Then stop it.

ELEANOR How? It's what I live for.

HENRY Rosamund, I loved you!

ELEANOR (*Calling*) John—Richard—Geoffrey.

HENRY Where's a priest? I'll do it. I'll show you. By Christ, I will. (*As* PHILIP, JOHN *and* GEOFFREY *enter from one side,* ALAIS *and* RICHARD *come in from the other*) Somebody dig me up a priest.

JOHN What for? What's happened?

ELEANOR Richard's getting married.

JOHN Now? He's getting married now?

ELEANOR I never cease to marvel at the quickness of your mind.

JOHN You can't hurt me, you bag of bile, no matter what you say. (*To* HENRY) But you can. Father, why?

HENRY Because I say so. (*To* GEOFFREY) You. Bring me a bishop.

ELEANOR (*As* GEOFFREY *starts to go*) Get old Durham. He's just down the hall. (GEOFFREY *exits. To* ALAIS) You'll make a lovely bride. I wonder if I'll cry.

ALAIS You sound as if you think it's going to happen.

ELEANOR And I do.

ALAIS He's only plotting. Can't you tell when Henry's plotting?

45

ELEANOR   Not this time.

ALAIS   He'll never give me up.

HENRY   You think I won't?

ALAIS   Because you told me so.

HENRY   You're not my Helen; I won't fight a war to save a face. We're done.

ALAIS   I don't believe you.

HENRY   Wait ten minutes.

GEOFFREY   (*Entering*)   I've sent word to Durham. He'll be waiting in the chapel.

HENRY   Good—let's get it over with.

ALAIS   Don't do this to me, Henry.

HENRY   (*To* RICHARD)   Take her.

ALAIS   No, wait. You don't want me, Richard.

HENRY   (*To* ALAIS)   Go to him.

ALAIS   (*As a procession forms around her*)   Not yet— (*To* PHILIP) I am your sister. Can't you find some pity for me? (*To* ELEANOR) Maman, you won't let this happen. (*Panic rising*) Henry, if you ever loved me— (*At a gesture from* HENRY, *the procession starts to move*) I won't do it. I won't say the words, not one of them. Henry, please. It makes no sense. Why give me up? What do you get? What are you gaining?

HENRY   Why, the Aquitaine, of course.

RICHARD   (*Stopping dead*)   What's that?

HENRY Your mother gets her freedom and I get the Aquitaine. (*To* ELEANOR) That is the proposition, isn't it? You did agree.

RICHARD (*To* ELEANOR) Of course she did. I knew, I knew it. It was all pretense. You used me. God, and I believed you. I believed it all.

ELEANOR I meant it all.

RICHARD No wedding. There will be no wedding.

HENRY But, my boy—

RICHARD Not at this price.

HENRY But Durham's waiting.

RICHARD She's not worth the Aquitaine.

HENRY You've simply got to marry her. It isn't much to ask. For my sake, Richard.

RICHARD Never.

HENRY But I've promised Philip. Think of my position.

RICHARD Damn the wedding and to hell with your position.

HENRY You don't dare defy me.

RICHARD Don't I?

HENRY (*To* PHILIP) You're the King of France, for goodness sake. Speak up. Do something.

RICHARD (*To* PHILIP) Make a threat, why don't you? Scare me.

PHILIP Dunce.

RICHARD Am I?

PHILIP He never meant to have the wedding.

HENRY Come again?

PHILIP You're good at rage. I like the way you play it.

HENRY Boy, don't ever call a king a liar to his face.

PHILIP I'm not a boy. To you or anybody.

HENRY Boy, you came here asking for a wedding or the Vexin back. By God, you don't get either one. It's no to both.

PHILIP You have a pact with France.

HENRY Then damn the document and damn the French. She'll never marry, not while I'm alive.

PHILIP Your life and never are two different times.

HENRY Not on my clock, boy.
        (PHILIP *exits*)

RICHARD Listen to the lion. Flash a yellow tooth and frighten me.

HENRY Don't spoil it, Richard. Take it like a good sport.

RICHARD How's your bad leg?

HENRY Better, thank you.

RICHARD And your back and all the rest of it. You're getting old. One day you'll have me once too often.

HENRY   When? I'm fifty now. My God, boy, I'm the oldest man I know. I've got a decade on the Pope. What's it to be? The broadsword when I'm eighty-five?

RICHARD   I'm not a second son. Not now. Your Henry's in the vault, you know.

HENRY   I know; I've seen him there.

RICHARD   I'll have the crown.

HENRY   You'll have what Daddy gives you.

RICHARD   I am next in line.

HENRY   To nothing.

RICHARD   Then we'll have the broadswords now.

HENRY   This minute?

RICHARD   On the battlefield.

HENRY   So we're at war.

RICHARD   Yes, we're at war. I have two thousand men at Poitiers.

HENRY   Can they hear you? Call and see who comes. You are as close to Poitiers as you're going to get.

RICHARD   You don't dare hold me prisoner.

HENRY   You're a king's son so I treat you with respect. You have the freedom of the castle.

RICHARD   You can't keep me here.

HENRY   Until we've all agreed that John comes next, I can and will.

RICHARD   The castle doesn't stand that holds me. Post your guards.
(*He exits*)

JOHN   My God, I'm king again. Fantastic. It's a miracle. (*To* GEOFFREY, *who joins him*) Are you happy for me, Geoff?

GEOFFREY (*As they exit together*)   I'm happy for us both.

ELEANOR   I came close, didn't I? (*To* ALAIS) I almost had my freedom and I almost had you for my son. I should have liked it, being free. (*To* HENRY) You played it nicely. You were good.

HENRY   I really was. I fooled you, didn't I? God, but I do love being king.

ELEANOR   Well, Henry, liege and lord, what happens now?

HENRY   I've no idea. I know I'm winning and I know I'll win but what the next move is— (*Looking at her closely*) You're not scared?

ELEANOR   No.

HENRY   I think you are.

ALAIS   I was. You mustn't play with feelings, Henry; not with mine.

HENRY   It wasn't possible to lose you. I must hold you dearer than I thought. (*To* ELEANOR) You've got your enigmatic face on. What's your mood, I wonder.

ELEANOR   Pure delight. I'm locked up with my sons: what mother wouldn't dream of that? (*She moves to go, then stops in the doorway*) One thing.

HENRY Yes?

ELEANOR May I watch you kiss her?

HENRY Can't you ever stop?

ELEANOR I watch you every night. I conjure it before I sleep.

HENRY Leave it at that.

ELEANOR My curiosity is intellectual: I want to see how accurate I am.

HENRY (*To* ALAIS) Forget the dragon in the doorway: come. (*Holding her*) Believe I love you, for I do. Believe I'm yours forever, for I am. Believe in my contentment and the joy you give me and believe— (*To* ELEANOR) You want more? (*Their eyes burn at each other. Then, turning slowly back to* ALAIS) I'm an old man in an empty place. Be with me.

(*They kiss.* ELEANOR *stands in the doorway, watching*)

Dim and blackout

ELEANOR's *chamber, shortly afterwards.* ELEANOR, *alone on stage, is seated at the table as the lights rise. A chest of jewels is on the table and she is feverishly covering herself with precious things.*

ELEANOR (*Putting on a great bib necklace*) How beautiful you make me. What might Solomon have sung had he seen this? (*Picking up a mirror, unable to look*) I can't. I'd turn to salt. (*Putting the mirror down*) I've lost again. I'm done, for now. Well—there'll be other Christmases. (*Picking up another elaborate necklace*) I'd hang you from the nipples but you'd shock the children. (*Putting it on*) They kissed sweetly, didn't they? I'll have him next time. I can wait. (*Picking up a crown*) Ah, there you are; my comfort and my company. We're locked in for another year: four seasons more. Oh, what a desolation, what a life's work. (*Putting it on as* GEOFFREY *enters*) Is it too much? Be sure to squint as you approach. You may be blinded by my beauty.

GEOFFREY Richard's raging all around the castle.

ELEANOR Is he? Why?

GEOFFREY He says it's got to do with being held a prisoner but I think he likes to rage.

ELEANOR   And John?

GEOFFREY   John's skipping after Richard, saying naughty things.

ELEANOR   And you?

GEOFFREY   I thought you might be lonely.

ELEANOR   (*Holding out the crown*) Here, Chancellor. Try it on for size.

GEOFFREY   Why do you think so little of me?

ELEANOR   Little? Never that. Whatever you are, you're not little.

GEOFFREY   I remember my third birthday. Not just pictures of the garden or the gifts, but who did what to whom and how it felt. My memory reaches back that far and never once can I remember anything from you or Father warmer than indifference. Why is that?

ELEANOR   I don't know.

GEOFFREY   That was not an easy question for me and I don't deserve an easy answer.

ELEANOR   There are times I think we loved none of our children.

GEOFFREY   Still too easy, don't you think?

ELEANOR   I'm weary and you want a simple answer and I haven't one. (*Starting to remove the jewelry*) I was thinking earlier of Peter Abélard. I was a queen of fifteen in those days and on dull afternoons I'd go watch Héloïse watch Abélard spread heresy like bonemeal in the palace gardens. Here the Seine and there the cypress

53

trees and how it bored me. Thought, pure thought, flashed clear as water all around me and all I could think about was how to make a Caesar of a monkish husband. I'd like to hear the old man talk again; I'd listen now. For my ambition's thin with age and all the mysteries are as plump as ever. (*Looking at* GEOFFREY) I read minds. In yours, a shapely hand is writing, "Clever Mother, what's your clever reason for this clever talk?" It isn't clever but you'll make it so. (*Patting his cheek*) I am so sick of all of you.

JOHN (*Entering*) I thought I'd come and gloat a little.

ELEANOR Mother's tired. Come stick pins tomorrow morning; I'll be more responsive then.

JOHN It's no fun goading anyone tonight.

ELEANOR Come, let me look at you. I'm full of looks this evening. I have looked a little in the mirror and I've read a passage in your brother's mind; what's there to see in you? A little me, a little Henry and a lot of someone I don't know. (*Turning away*) Oh, John . . .

RICHARD (*Entering*) The bastard's boxed us up.

ELEANOR What's that, dear?

RICHARD We're his prisoners, if that interests you.

ELEANOR Why should it? I'm his prisoner anyway.

RICHARD I've got to get to Poitiers. Henry wants a war, I'll give him one.

ELEANOR I don't see how.

RICHARD You seem to take that calmly.

54

ELEANOR Well?

RICHARD It was—correct me if I'm wrong, but it was my impression that you wanted Henry's throne for me.

ELEANOR We've lost it this time, Richard. We can't win.

RICHARD You think I'm finished, do you?

ELEANOR So I do. I've suffered more defeats than you have teeth. I know one when it happens to me. Take your wormwood like a good boy. Swallow it and go to bed.

RICHARD I will be king.

ELEANOR And so you will. But not this year—and what's it matter to me anyway? The world stops when I die.

RICHARD Yours does; mine doesn't.

ELEANOR Leave it, Richard. Let it go for now. I have.

RICHARD I can't.

JOHN It's not so hard. Try saying after me: John wins, I lose.

RICHARD What if John died?

JOHN What's that?

RICHARD What if he left us suddenly.

JOHN You wouldn't dare.

RICHARD (*Going for his dagger*) Why on earth wouldn't I?

JOHN A knife—he's got a knife.

55

ELEANOR   Of course he has a knife. He always has a knife.
We all have knives. It is eleven eighty-three and we're
barbarians. How clear we make it. Oh, my piglets, we're
the origins of war. Not history's forces nor the times
nor justice nor the lack of it nor causes nor religions nor
ideas nor kinds of government nor any other thing. We
are the killers; we breed war. We carry it, like syphilis,
inside. Dead bodies rot in field and stream because the
living ones are rotten. For the love of God, can't we love
one another just a little? That's how peace begins. We
have so much to love each other for. We have such possibilities, my children; we could change the world.

GEOFFREY   And while we hugged each other, what would
Philip do?

JOHN   Oh good God—Philip. We're supposed to start a
war. If Father finds out, I'll be ruined.

GEOFFREY   Steady, John; don't panic.

JOHN   Some advisor you are.

GEOFFREY   Don't do anything without me. Let me handle
it.

JOHN   If you're so smart, why am I always doing something dumb?
      (He exits)

ELEANOR   (Alive again) Well, Geoffrey. He's made a
pact with Philip. You advised John into making war.
That peerless boy; he's disinherited himself. When
Henry finds out, when I tell him what John's done— I
need a little time. Can you keep John away from Philip
till I say so?

56

GEOFFREY Anything you say.
(*He exits*)

ELEANOR (*To* RICHARD) I want you out of here before
this breaks. And that needs Philip. He has soldiers with
him if he'll use them. Go to him, be desperate, promise
anything: the Vexin, Brittany. Then once you're free
and John is out of favor, we'll make further plans.

RICHARD You talk to Philip. You're the diplomat; you see
him.

ELEANOR You're a friend. You know him; I don't.
Quickly now. (*He moves to exit*) And, Richard. (*He
turns in the doorway*) Promise anything. (*He exits*) I
haven't lost, it isn't over. Oh, I've got the old man this
time. The damn fool thinks he loves John, he believes
it. That's where the knife goes in. Knives, knives . . .
it was a fine thought, wasn't it? Oh, Henry, we have
done a big thing badly. (*Looking for her mirror*) Where's
that mirror? I am Eleanor and I can look at anything.
(*Gazing into the mirror*) My, what a lovely girl. How
could her king have left her?

Dim and blackout

SCENE 6

PHILIP's *chamber, immediately following. It is a gracious room, its back wall lined with tapestries. A canopy bed, the curtains closed, stands at one side. A pair of chairs sit, one at each side of a low table on which there are two goblets and a wine decanter.*

As the lights rise, PHILIP *is preparing for bed. He turns as* GEOFFREY, *calling his name, comes skidding into the room.*

GEOFFREY   Philip, Philip—is John here?

PHILIP   Here? In my room?

GEOFFREY   Come on, Philip; this is me.

PHILIP   I've been expecting him.

GEOFFREY   The whole thing breaks tonight; we've reached the end of it.

PHILIP   If that's a warning, thank you.

GEOFFREY   What if it's an offer?

PHILIP   "What if" is a game for scholars: what if angels sat on pinheads?

GEOFFREY   What if I were king?

PHILIP   It's your game, Geoff; you play it.

GEOFFREY   All of England's land in France, from Normandy down to the Spanish border, once I'm king.

PHILIP   All that. What could I do that's worth all that?

GEOFFREY   By morning I can be the chosen son. The crown can come to me. But once it does, once Henry's favor falls my way, the war begins.

PHILIP   We have so many wars. Which one is this?

GEOFFREY   The one that Richard, John and Eleanor will make. I'll have to fight to keep what Henry, in his rage, is going to give me.

PHILIP   Yes, you will.

GEOFFREY   That's why I need you, Philip. Will you fight with me against them all?

PHILIP   Against them all?

GEOFFREY   Don't tell me it's a risk. I wouldn't hand you half of France to fight an easy war.

PHILIP   I wouldn't want you for an enemy.

GEOFFREY   Are we allies, then?

PHILIP   We were born to be.

GEOFFREY   I should say something solemn but I haven't time. I'm off to Father with the news that John's a traitor. After that—

JOHN (*Bursting from behind the tapestry*)   You stink, you know that? You're a stinker and you stink.

GEOFFREY Come on. We're finished here.

JOHN I'll kill you. Where's a dagger?

GEOFFREY Hush, John, or you'll spoil everything.

JOHN A sword, a spear, a candlestick. (*Reaching for a candlestick*) It's lights out, stinker.

GEOFFREY (*Stopping him*) Dumb. If you're a prince, there's hope for every ape in Africa. I had you saved. I wasn't on my way to Father—but he was. He would have gone to Henry and betrayed you. Look: it's in his face.

JOHN (*Looking at* PHILIP *in dismay*) Oh. It's true. I don't know who my friends are.

RICHARD (*Offstage, calling from a distance*) Philip.

GEOFFREY (*Indicating the tapestry*) May we?

PHILIP That's what tapestries are for.

JOHN (*As* GEOFFREY *disappears, with him, behind the tapestry*) I've ruined everything. I'll never learn.

PHILIP Is someone there? I heard my name.

RICHARD (*Entering*) I called it.

PHILIP Richard. Hello, Richard.

RICHARD You're halfway to bed. I'll wait for morning.

PHILIP Come in.

RICHARD Mother sent me.

PHILIP Come in anyway. (*Filling glasses from the decanter*) Our alchemists have stumbled on the art of boiling burgundy. It turns to steam and when it cools we call it brandywine.

RICHARD   I'm Henry's prisoner.

PHILIP   So you said you'd go to war and Henry drew the drawbridge on you.

RICHARD   Do you find that charming?

PHILIP   No.

RICHARD   Then why the charming smile?

PHILIP   I thought, I can't think why, of when you were in Paris last. Can it be two whole years ago?

RICHARD   It can. I need an army, Philip.

PHILIP   (*Handing him the brandy*)   It will take the cold away.

RICHARD   I must have soldiers.

PHILIP   Have I aged? Do I seem older to you? They've been two fierce years: I've studied and I've trained to be a king.

RICHARD   I'll have your answer—yes or no.

PHILIP   (*Cold*)   You'll have it when I give it. (*Warm again*) See? I've changed. I'm not the boy you taught to hunt two years ago. Remember? Racing after boar, you flying first, me scrambling after, all day into dusk—

RICHARD   (*Turning to leave*)   I'll try another time.

PHILIP   Don't go.

RICHARD   I must know: will you help me?

PHILIP Sit and we'll discuss it. (RICHARD *sits*) You never write.

RICHARD To anyone.

PHILIP Why should I make you King of England? Aren't I better off with John or Geoffrey? Why have you to fight when I could have the cretin or the fiend?

RICHARD Would we fight?

PHILIP We're fighting now. (*Terminating the interview*) Good night.

RICHARD You're still a boy.

PHILIP In some ways. Which way did you have in mind?

RICHARD You haven't asked how much you're worth to me.

PHILIP You'll tell me.

RICHARD You can have the Vexin back.

PHILIP And what else?

RICHARD All of Brittany.

PHILIP That's Geoffrey's.

RICHARD Does that matter?

PHILIP Possibly to Geoffrey. And what else?

RICHARD That's all your help is worth.

PHILIP And in return, what do you want from me?

RICHARD Two thousand soldiers.

Robert Preston as HENRY II and Rosemary Harris as
ELEANOR OF AQUITAINE.

PHILIP   And what else?

RICHARD   Five hundred knights on horse.

PHILIP   And what else?

RICHARD   Arms and siege equipment.

PHILIP   And what else?

RICHARD   I never wrote because I thought you'd never answer. (PHILIP *says nothing*) You got married.

PHILIP   Does that make a difference?

RICHARD   Doesn't it?

PHILIP   I've spent two years on every street in hell.

RICHARD   That's odd: I didn't see you there. (PHILIP *takes* RICHARD's *hand. They start moving to the bed*) You haven't said you love me.

PHILIP   When the time comes.

HENRY   (*Offstage, calling*) Philip.

RICHARD   Don't go.

PHILIP   Hush.
        (*He opens the bed curtains*)

RICHARD   Philip . . . (*Climbing through the curtains*) Hurry.

HENRY   (*Still offstage*) Philip, lad.

PHILIP   (*Closing the curtains*) Is someone there?

HENRY   (*Entering*) I am. It's not too late at night?

PHILIP   I've been expecting you.

HENRY   Oh, have you?

PHILIP   (*Indicating the glasses, his and* RICHARD's)   See —two glasses. I did hope you'd come.

HENRY   Good; we can't leave negotiations where they are. I've seen more royal rooms. Poor Chinon wasn't meant to sleep so many kings. I keep looking for your father in you.

PHILIP   (*Pouring brandy*)   He's not there.

HENRY   I miss him. Has Richard or the Queen been here to see you?

PHILIP   Does it matter? If they haven't yet, they will.

HENRY   I want to reach a settlement. I left you with too little earlier.

PHILIP   Yes; nothing is too little.

HENRY   I am sorry you're not fonder of me, lad. Your father always said, "Be fond of stronger men."

PHILIP   No wonder he loved everyone.

HENRY   They'll offer you whole provinces to fight me.

PHILIP   Shocking. My advice to you is discipline your children.

HENRY   I came here to offer peace.

PHILIP   Piss on your peace.

HENRY   Your father would have wept.

PHILIP   My father was a weeper.

HENRY   Fight me and you'll lose.

PHILIP I can't lose, Henry. I have time. Just look at you. Great heavy arms—they'd crush me like a leaf of lettuce. But each year they get a little heavier. The sand goes pit-pat in the glass. I'm in no hurry, Henry. I've got time.

HENRY Suppose I hurry things along? What if I say that England is at war with France?

PHILIP Then France surrenders. I don't have to fight to win. Take all you want—this county, that one. You won't keep it long.

HENRY What kind of courage have you got?

PHILIP The tidal kind: it comes and goes.

HENRY By God, I'd love to turn you loose on Eleanor. More brandywine?

PHILIP You recognize it?

HENRY They were boiling it in Ireland before the snakes left. Well, things look a little bleak for Henry, don't they? You'll say yes to Richard when he comes; arms, soldiers, anything he asks for.

PHILIP I'd be foolish not to.

HENRY And withdraw it all before the battle ever started.

PHILIP Wouldn't you, in my place?

HENRY Why fight Henry when his sons will do it for you?

PHILIP Yes, exactly.

HENRY You've got promise, lad. That's first-class thinking.

PHILIP Thank you, sir.

HENRY (*Emptying his glass*) Good night.

PHILIP (*Uncertain for the first time*) Good night? You're going? (HENRY *nods benignly*) But we haven't settled anything.

HENRY We open Christmas packages at noon. Till then.

PHILIP You can't be finished with me.

HENRY But I am. And it's been very satisfactory.

PHILIP What's so satisfactory?

HENRY Winning is. I did just win. Surely you noticed.

PHILIP Not a thing. You haven't won a damn thing.

HENRY I've found out the way your mind works and the kind of man you are. I know your plans and expectations. You have burbled every bit of strategy you've got. I know exactly what you will do and exactly what you won't. And I've told you exactly nothing. To these aged eyes, boy, that's what winning looks like. *Dormez bien.*

PHILIP One time, when I was very small, I watched some soldiers take their dinner pig and truss it up and put the thing, alive and kicking, on the fire. That's the sound I'm going to hear from you.

HENRY And I thought you lacked passion.

PHILIP You—you made my father nothing. You were always better. You bullied him, you bellied with his wife, you beat him down in every war, you twisted every treaty, you played mock-the-monk and then you made him love you for it. I was there: his last words went to you.

HENRY   He was a loving man and you learned nothing of it.

PHILIP   I learned how much fathers live in sons. A king like you has policy prepared on everything. What's the official line on sodomy? How stands the Crown on boys who do with boys?

HENRY   Richard finds his way into so many legends. Let's hear yours and see how it compares.

PHILIP   He found me first when I was fifteen. We were hunting. It was nearly dark. I lost my way. My horse fell. I was thrown. I woke to Richard touching me. He asked me if I loved him—Philip, do you love me?— and I told him yes.

HENRY   I've heard much better.

PHILIP   You know why I told him yes? So one day I could tell you all about it. You cannot imagine what that yes cost. Or perhaps you can. Imagine snuggling to a chancred whore and, bending back your lips in something like a smile, saying, "Yes I love you and I find you beautiful." I don't know how I did it.

RICHARD   (*Charging from the bed*)   No! It wasn't like that.

PHILIP   But it was.

RICHARD   You loved me.

PHILIP   Never.

RICHARD   Get your sword. You've got one. Pick it up.

PHILIP   (*To* HENRY)   He's your responsibility; you talk to him.

RICHARD (*To* HENRY) Get out. Please! I don't want you here.

HENRY It's no great joy to be here.

RICHARD So the royal corkscrew finds me twisted, does he?

HENRY I'll go tell your mother: she'll be pleased.

RICHARD She knows: she sent me.

HENRY How completely hers you are.

RICHARD You've had four sons. Who do you claim? Not Henry? Not my buried brother. Not that monument to muck, that epic idiot, oh, surely not.

HENRY The boy is dead.

RICHARD Let's praise him, then. Who can forget his roquefort smile, his absent brow, those apey eyes, that spoon-edged mind? Why him? Why him and never me?

HENRY He was the oldest. He came first.

RICHARD Christ, Henry, is that all?

HENRY You went with Eleanor.

RICHARD You never called for me. You never said my name. I would have walked or crawled. I'd have done anything.

HENRY It's not my fault. I won't be blamed.

RICHARD I only wanted you.

HENRY No—it's my crown. You want my kingdom.

RICHARD Keep your kingdom.

HENRY That I will.

RICHARD I hope it kills you.

HENRY I thank God I have another son. Thank God for John.

GEOFFREY (*Stepping from behind the tapestry*) Who shall we thank for Geoffrey? (*To* HENRY) You don't think much of me.

HENRY Much? I don't think of you at all.

GEOFFREY Nurse used to say I had your hands; I might have more of you. Try seeing me. I haven't Richard's military skill; but he was here betraying you, not I. I haven't John's I don't know what—God knows what you can see in John—and he's betrayed you, too. There's only me.

HENRY You think I'd ever make you king?

GEOFFREY You'll make me king because I'm all you've got. (*Indicating* RICHARD) I was to be his chancellor. Ask him why.

HENRY I've heard enough.

GEOFFREY For moving John to treason.

HENRY I don't doubt he offered, I don't doubt you tried and I don't doubt John loves me.

GEOFFREY Like a glutton loves his lunch.
    (*He pulls the tapestry from in front of* JOHN)

JOHN (*To* GEOFFREY) You turd.

HENRY Well, John?

69

JOHN It isn't what you think.

HENRY What do I think?

JOHN What Geoffrey said. I wouldn't plot against you, ever.

HENRY I know; you're a good boy.

JOHN Can I go now, please? It's late. I ought to be in bed.

HENRY You fool.

JOHN Me? What have I done now?

HENRY Couldn't you wait? Couldn't you trust me? It was all yours. Couldn't you believe that?

JOHN Will you listen to the grief?

HENRY Who do you think I built this kingdom for?

JOHN Me? Daddy did it all for me? When can I have it, Daddy? Not until we bury you?

HENRY You're just like them. And after all I've given you.

JOHN I got it; I know what you gave.

HENRY I loved you.

JOHN You're a cold and bloody bastard, you are, and you don't love anything.

GEOFFREY I'm it, I'm all that's left. Here, Father; here I am.

HENRY My life, when it is written, will read better than it lived. Henry Fitz-Empress, first Plantagenet, a king at twenty-one, the ablest soldier of an able time. He led men well, he cared for justice when he could and ruled,

70

for thirty years, a state as great as Charlemagne's. He married, out of love, a woman out of legend. Not in Alexandria or Rome or Camelot has there been such a queen. She bore him many children—but no sons. King Henry had no sons. He had three whiskered things but he disowned them. You're not mine. We're not connected. I deny you. None of you will get my crown. I leave you nothing and I wish you plague. May all your children breech and die. (*Moving unsteadily toward the door*) My boys are gone. I've lost my boys. (*Stopping, glaring up*) You dare to damn me, do you? Well, I damn you back. God damn you. All my boys are gone. I've lost my boys. Oh Jesus, all my boys.

Blackout and curtain

ACT TWO

ACT TWO

HENRY's *chamber, late at night. It is a large room, un-
adorned and without ornament. There is a plain hard bed,
an armchair and a charcoal brazier. As the curtain rises,*
ALAIS, *dressed for bed, is crouching by the brazier, adding
spices to a pot of mulled wine.*

ALAIS (*Singing softly*)
 The Christmas wine is in the pot,
 The Christmas coals are red.
 I'll spend the day
 The lovers' way,
 Unwrapping all my gifts in bed.
  (ELEANOR *appears behind her*)
 The Christmas goose is on the spit,
 The Christmas . . .
  (*She senses someone and turns*)

ELEANOR No one else is caroling tonight. It might as
 well be Lent. When I was little, Christmas was a time
 of great confusion for me: the Holy Land had two kings,
 God and Uncle Raymond, and I never knew whose birthday we were celebrating.

ALAIS Henry isn't here.

ELEANOR Good; we can talk behind his back.

75

ALAIS   He's outside, walking.

ELEANOR   In this cold?

ALAIS   He'll never notice it. What happened?

ELEANOR   Don't you know?

ALAIS   He came and stood awhile by the fire and went away. You would have liked the way he looked.

ELEANOR   There was a scene with beds and tapestries and many things got said. Spiced wine; I'd forgotten Henry liked it. May I stay?

ALAIS   It's your room just as much as mine: we're both in residence.

ELEANOR   Packed in, like the poor, three to a bed.

ALAIS   Did you love Henry—ever?

ELEANOR   Ever? Back before the flood?

ALAIS   As long ago as Rosamund.

ELEANOR   Ah, that's pre-history, lamb; there are no written records or survivors.

ALAIS   There are pictures. She was prettier than you.

ELEANOR   Oh, much. Her eyes, in certain light, were violet and all her teeth were even. That's a rare fair feature, even teeth. She smiled to excess but she chewed with real distinction.

ALAIS   And you hate her even now.

ELEANOR   No, but I did. He put her in my place, you see, and that was very hard. Like you, she headed Henry's table; that's my chair.

ALAIS And so you had her poisoned.

ELEANOR That's a folk tale. Oh, I prayed for her to drop
and sang a little when she did but even Circe had her
limits. No, I never poisoned Rosamund. Why aren't you
happy? Henry's keeping you. You must be cleverer than
I am.

ALAIS Green becomes you. You must always wear it.

ELEANOR Are you dressing me in envy?

ALAIS I've tried feeling pity for you but it keeps on turning into something else.

ELEANOR Why pity?

ALAIS You love Henry but you love his kingdom, too. You
look at him and you see cities, acreage, coastline, taxes.
All I see is Henry. Leave him to me, can't you?

ELEANOR But I left him years ago.

ALAIS You are untouchable. And I thought I could move
you. Were you always like this? Years ago, when I was
young and worshiped you, is this what you were like?

ELEANOR Most likely. Child, I'm finished and I've come
to give him anything he asks for.

ALAIS Do you know what I should like for Christmas? I
should like to see you suffer.

ELEANOR (*Nodding*) Alais, just for you.

ALAIS (*Throwing herself into* ELEANOR's *arms*) Maman,
oh, Maman.

77

ELEANOR (*Singing softly*)
  The Christmas wine will make you warm—
Don't shiver, child.

ALAIS I'm not.

ELEANOR
  The Christmas logs will glow.
There's Christmas cheer and comfort here—
Is that you crying?

ALAIS *Non, Maman.*

ELEANOR Hold close and never let me go.
    (HENRY *appears behind them*)

HENRY The sky is pocked with stars. What eyes the wise
men must have had to spot a new one in so many.

ELEANOR You look cold.

ALAIS I've mulled some wine.

HENRY I wonder, were there fewer stars then—I don't
know. I fancy there's a mystery in it. (ALAIS *hands him
a cup of wine*) What's this?

ALAIS Warm wine.

HENRY Why, so it is. (*Cupping her face in his hands*)
You are as beautiful as I remembered. (*Briskly*) Off to
bed. My widow wants to see me.

ALAIS Let me stay.

HENRY Wait up for me. I won't be long.

ALAIS She came to find out what your plans are.

HENRY I know that.

ALAIS She wants you back.

HENRY (*To* ELEANOR) Old as I am?

ELEANOR Old as you are.

ALAIS Oh, eat each other up for all I care. (*She starts to go, then stops and turns*) I'm an orphan and I'll never have a husband and my lover's wife has fangs for teeth and everybody's going to die. We've got no Romans and no Christians but the rest of the arena, that we have.
(*She exits*)

ELEANOR I'm rather proud; I taught her all the rhetoric she knows.

HENRY (*Pouring wine for her*) So you want me back.

ELEANOR She thinks I do. She thinks the need for loving never stops.

HENRY She's got a point. I marvel at you: after all these years, still like a democratic drawbridge, going down for everybody.

ELEANOR (*He gives her wine*) At my age, there's not much traffic any more.

HENRY To your interminable health. (*He drinks*) Well, wife, what's on your mind?

ELEANOR Oh, Henry, we have made a mess of it.

HENRY Yes, haven't we.

ELEANOR Could we have done it worse?

HENRY You look like Doomsday.

ELEANOR   Late nights do that to me. Am I puffy?

HENRY   Possibly: it's hard to tell; there's all that natural sag.

ELEANOR   I've just seen Richard.

HENRY   Splendid boy.

ELEANOR   He says you fought.

HENRY   We always do.

ELEANOR   It's his impression that you plan to disinherit them.

HENRY   I fancy I'll relent. Don't you?

ELEANOR   I don't much care. In fact, I wonder, Henry, if I care for anything. I wonder if I'm hungry out of habit and if all my lusts, like passions in a poem, aren't really recollections.

HENRY   I could listen to you lie for hours. So your lust is rusty. Gorgeous.

ELEANOR   I'm so tired, Henry.

HENRY   Sleep, then. Sleep and dream of me with croutons. *Henri à la mode de Caen.*

ELEANOR   Henry, stop it.

HENRY   Eleanor, I haven't started.

ELEANOR   What is it you want? You want the day? You've carried it. It's yours. I'm yours.

HENRY   My what? You are my what?

ELEANOR   Your anything at all. You want my name on

paper? I'll sign anything. You want the Aquitaine for John? It's John's. It's his, it's yours, it's anybody's. Take it.

HENRY In exchange for what?

ELEANOR For nothing, for a little quiet, for an end to this, for God's sake sail me back to England, lock me up and lose the key and let me be alone. (HENRY *applauds, louder and louder*) You have my oath. I give my word. (*The applause stops. Sinking, bone-weary, into the chair*) Oh. Well. Well, well.

HENRY Would you like a pillow? Footstool? What about a shawl? (*She stares dully through him*) Your oaths are all profanities. Your word's a curse. Your name on paper is a waste of pulp. I'm vilifying you, for God's sake. Pay attention. (*No response*) Eleanor! (*She reaches out, takes his hand and kisses it*) Don't do that.
     (*She drops the hand*)

ELEANOR (*Flatly, from far away*) Like any thinking person, I should like to think there was—I don't care whose or which—some God. Not out of fear: death is a lark; it's life that stings. But if there were some God, then I'd exist in his imagination, like Antigone in Sophocles'. I'd have no contradictions, no confusions, no waste parts or misplaced elements and then, oh, Henry, then I'd make some sense. I'd be a queen in Arcady and not an animal in chaos. How, from where we started, did we ever reach this Christmas?

HENRY Step by step.

ELEANOR What happens to me now?

HENRY   That's lively curiosity from such a dead cat. If you want to know my plans, just ask me.

ELEANOR   Conquer China, sack the Vatican or take the veil; I'm not among the ones who give a damn. Just let me sign my lands to John and go to bed.

HENRY   No, you're too kind. I can't accept.

ELEANOR   Oh, come on, man. I'll sign the thing in blood or spit or bright blue ink. Let's have it done.

HENRY   Let's not. No, I don't think I want your signature on anything.

ELEANOR   You don't?

HENRY   Dear God, the pleasure I still get from goading you.

ELEANOR   You don't want John to have my provinces?

HENRY   Bull's eye.

ELEANOR   I can't bear you when you're smug.

HENRY   I know, I know.

ELEANOR   You don't want Richard and you don't want John.

HENRY   You've grasped it.

ELEANOR   All right, let me have it. Level me. What do you want?

HENRY   A new wife.

ELEANOR   Oh.

HENRY Aesthete and poetaster that you are, you worship beauty and simplicity. I worship with you. Down with all that's ugly and complex, like frogs or pestilence or our relationship. I ask you, what's more beautiful and simple than a new wife?

ELEANOR So I'm to be annulled. Well, will the Pope annul me, do you think?

HENRY The Pontiff owes me one Pontificate; I think he will.

ELEANOR Out Eleanor, in Alais. Why?

HENRY Why? Not since Caesar, seeing Brutus with the bloody dagger in his hand, asked, "You, too?" has there been a dumber question.

ELEANOR I'll stand by it. Why?

HENRY A new wife, wife, will bear me sons.

ELEANOR That is the single thing of which I should have thought you had enough.

HENRY I want a son.

ELEANOR Whatever for? Why, we could populate a country town with country girls who've borne you sons. How many is it? Help me count the bastards.

HENRY All my sons are bastards.

ELEANOR You really mean to do it.

HENRY Lady love, with all my heart.

ELEANOR Your sons are part of you.

HENRY Like warts and goiters—and I'm having them removed.

ELEANOR We made them. They're our boys.

HENRY I know. And good God, look at them. Young Henry: vain, deceitful, weak and cowardly. The only patriotic thing he ever did was die.

ELEANOR I thought you loved him most.

HENRY I did. And Geoffrey: there's a masterpiece. He isn't flesh: he's a device; he's wheels and gears.

ELEANOR Well, every family has one.

HENRY But not four. Then Johnny. Was his latest treason your idea?

ELEANOR John has so few ideas; no, I can't bring myself to claim it.

HENRY I have caught him lying and I've said he's young. I've seen him cheating and I've thought he's just a boy. I've watched him steal and whore and whip his servants and he's not a child. He is the man we've made him.

ELEANOR Don't share John with me; he's your accomplishment.

HENRY And Richard's yours. How could you send him off to deal with Philip?

ELEANOR I was tired. I was busy. They were friends.

HENRY Eleanor, he was the best. The strongest, bravest, handsomest and from the cradle on you cradled him. I never had a chance.

ELEANOR You never wanted one.

HENRY How do you know? You took him. Separation from your husband you could bear. But not your boy.

ELEANOR Whatever I have done, you made me do.

HENRY You threw me out of bed for Richard.

ELEANOR Not until you threw me out for Rosamund.

HENRY It's not that simple. I won't have it be that simple.

ELEANOR I adored you.

HENRY Never.

ELEANOR I still do.

HENRY Of all the lies, that one is the most terrible.

ELEANOR I know: that's why I saved it up for now. (*They throw themselves into each other's arms*) Oh, Henry, we have mangled everything we've touched.

HENRY Deny us what you will, we have done that. And all for Rosamund.

ELEANOR No, you were right: it is too simple. Life, if it's like anything at all, is like an avalanche. To blame the little ball of snow that starts it all, to say it is the cause, is just as true as it is meaningless.

HENRY Do you remember when we met?

ELEANOR Down to the hour and the color of your stockings.

HENRY I could hardly see you for the sunlight.

ELEANOR It was raining but no matter.

HENRY   There was very little talk as I recall it.

ELEANOR   Very little.

HENRY   I had never seen such beauty—and I walked right
up and touched it. God, where did I find the gall to do
that?

ELEANOR   In my eyes.

HENRY   I loved you.
   (*They kiss*)

ELEANOR   No annulment.

HENRY   What?

ELEANOR   There will be no annulment.

HENRY   Will there not?

ELEANOR   No; I'm afraid you'll have to do without.

HENRY   Well . . . it was just a whim.

ELEANOR   I'm so relieved. I didn't want to lose you.

HENRY   Out of curiosity, as intellectual to intellectual,
how in the name of bleeding Jesus can you lose me? Do
you ever see me? Am I ever with you? Ever near you?
Am I ever anywhere but somewhere else?

ELEANOR   I'm not concerned about your geographical lo-
cation.

HENRY   Do we write? Do I send messages? Do dinghies
bearing gifts float up the Thames to you? Are you remembered?

ELEANOR   You are.

HENRY You're no part of me. We do not touch at any point. How can you lose me?

ELEANOR Can't you feel the chains?

HENRY You know enough to know I can't be stopped.

ELEANOR But I don't have to stop you; I have only to delay you. Every enemy you have has friends in Rome. We'll cost you time.

HENRY What is this? I'm not moldering; my paint's not peeling off. I'm good for years.

ELEANOR How many years? Suppose I hold you back for one; I can—it's possible. Suppose your first son dies; ours did—it's possible. Suppose you're daughtered next; we were—that, too, is possible. How old is Daddy then? What kind of spindly, rickets-ridden, milky, semi-witted, wizened, dim-eyed, gammy-handed, limpy line of things will you beget?

HENRY It's sweet of you to care.

ELEANOR And when you die, which is regrettable but necessary, what will happen to frail Alais and her pruney prince? You can't think Richard's going to wait for your grotesque to grow?

HENRY You wouldn't let him do a thing like that?

ELEANOR Let him? I'd push him through the nursery door.

HENRY You're not that cruel.

ELEANOR Don't fret. We'll wait until you're dead to do it.

HENRY Eleanor, what do you want?

ELEANOR Just what you want: a king for a son. You can make more. I can't. You think I want to disappear? One son is all I've got and you can blot him out and call me cruel. For these ten years you've lived with everything I've lost and loved another woman through it all. And I'm cruel. I could peel you like a pear and God himself would call it justice. Nothing I could do to you is wanton; nothing is too much.

HENRY I will die sometime soon. One day I'll duck too slow and at Westminster, they'll sing out *Vivat Rex* for someone else. I beg you, let it be a son of mine.

ELEANOR I am not moved to tears.

HENRY I have no sons.

ELEANOR You've got too many sons. You don't need more.

HENRY Well, wish me luck. I'm off.

ELEANOR To Rome?

HENRY That's where they keep the Pope.

ELEANOR You don't dare go.

HENRY Say that again at noon, you'll say it to my horse's ass. Lamb, I'll be rid of you by Easter: you can count your reign in days.

ELEANOR You go to Rome, we'll rise against you.

HENRY Who will?

ELEANOR Richard, Geoffrey, John and Eleanor of Aquitaine.

HENRY The day those stout hearts band together is the day that pigs get wings.

ELEANOR   There'll be pork in the treetops come the morning. Don't you see? You've given them a common cause: new sons. You leave the country and you've lost it.

HENRY   All of you at once.

ELEANOR   And Philip, too. He'd join us.

HENRY   Yes, he would.

ELEANOR   Now how's your trip to Rome?

HENRY   You'd truly do this to me?

ELEANOR   Oh, I've got you, got you, got you.

HENRY   Should I take a thousand men-at-arms to Rome or is that showy?

ELEANOR   Bluff away. I love it.

HENRY   Ah, poor thing. How can I break the news? You've just miscalculated.

ELEANOR   Have I? How?

HENRY   You should have lied to me. You should have promised to be good while I was gone. I would have let your three boys loose. They could have fought me then.

ELEANOR   You wouldn't keep your sons locked up here?

HENRY   Why the devil wouldn't I?

ELEANOR   You don't dare.

HENRY   Why not? What's to stop me? Let them sit in Chinon for a while.

ELEANOR   No; I forbid it!

HENRY   She forbids it!

ELEANOR   Did your father sleep with me, or didn't he?

HENRY   No doubt you're going to tell me that he did.

ELEANOR   Would it upset you?

HENRY   What about the thousand men? I say be gaudy and to hell with it.

ELEANOR   Don't leave me, Henry. I'm at rock bottom, I'll do anything to keep you.

HENRY   I think you think you mean it.

ELEANOR   Ask for something.

HENRY   Eleanor, we're past it; years past.

ELEANOR   Test me. Name an act.

HENRY   There isn't one.

ELEANOR   About my fornication with your father—

HENRY   Yes, there is. You can expire.

ELEANOR   You first, old man. I only hope I'm there to watch. You're so afraid of dying. You're so scared of it.

HENRY   Poor Eleanor; if only she had lied.

ELEANOR   She did. She said she never loved your father.

HENRY   I can always count on you.

ELEANOR   I've never touched you without thinking, "Geoffrey, Geoffrey."

HENRY   When you hurt me, I'll cry out.

ELEANOR I've put more horns on you than Louis ever wore.

HENRY Am I supposed to care?

ELEANOR I'll kill you if you leave me.

HENRY You can try.

ELEANOR I loved your father's body. He was beautiful.

HENRY It never happened.

ELEANOR I can see his body now. Shall I describe it?

HENRY Eleanor, I hope you die.

ELEANOR His arms were rough, with scars here—

HENRY Stop it!

ELEANOR I can feel his arms. I feel them.

HENRY AAH!

ELEANOR What's that? Have I hurt you?

HENRY Oh my God, I'm going to be sick.

ELEANOR (*Hurling it after him as he exits*) We did it. You were in the next room when he did it! (*He is gone. Bleakly, in desolation*) Well, what family doesn't have its ups and downs? (*At the brazier, spreading her hands over it*) It's cold. I can't feel anything. (*Huddling close to the coals*) Not anything at all. (*Hugging herself, arms around tight*) We couldn't go back, could we, Henry?

Dim and blackout

SCENE 2

ALAIS's *chamber, at dawn.* ALAIS, *dressed for bed as we saw her last, sits deeply asleep in a chair.* HENRY *enters, moves to the window, and throws back the curtain. His spirits are too high; the man is feverish and a little frightening.*

HENRY   Get up, wake up, it's morning.

ALAIS *(Startled)* Henry?

HENRY   When the King is off his ass, nobody sleeps.

ALAIS   What's wrong?

HENRY   We're packing up and moving out.

ALAIS   Is there a war? What's happened?

HENRY   Merry Christmas.

ALAIS   Henry, what's the matter?

HENRY   Nothing, for a change; would you believe it?

ALAIS   Where've you been all night?

HENRY   You know what a *mesnie* is? It's a train, an entourage. It's made of soldiers, cooks and clerics, wagons,

92

barrows, linen, treasure, chickens, butts of wine and spices. I've been all night making one.

ALAIS   What for?

HENRY   We're off to Rome to see the Pope.

ALAIS   He's excommunicated you again.

HENRY   He's going to set me free. I'm having Eleanor annulled. The nation will be shocked to learn our marriage wasn't consummated.

ALAIS   What happened last night when I left?

HENRY   We hugged and kissed a little.

ALAIS   Oh, be serious.

HENRY   And then, I told her you and I were getting married.

ALAIS   Are we?

HENRY   By the Pope himself.

ALAIS   You mean it?

HENRY   Shall I kneel?

ALAIS   It's not another trick?

HENRY   The bridal party's drilling on the cobblestones.

ALAIS   She loves you, Henry.

HENRY   See for yourself.

ALAIS   She'll find a way to stop us.

HENRY   How? She won't be here. We're launching her for

Salisbury Tower when the winds change. She'll be barging down the River Vienne by lunchtime.

ALAIS If she doesn't stop us, Richard will.

HENRY Suppose I do the worrying.

ALAIS He won't like losing me.

HENRY He's lost a damn sight more than you. I've corked him up.

ALAIS You've what?

HENRY He's in the cellar with his brothers and the wine. The royal boys are aging with the royal port. You haven't said "yes." Would you like a formal declaration? (*Kneeling, giving her his profile*) There—my finest angle; it's on all the coins. Sad Alais, will you marry me?

ALAIS I can't believe it.

HENRY Be my Queen.

ALAIS I never hoped for this. I mean, I always hoped but never thought—I mean—

HENRY We'll love each other and you'll give me sons.

ALAIS I don't know what I mean.

HENRY Let's have five; we'll do Eleanor one better. Why, I'll even call the first one Louis if you like. Louis le Premier: how's that for a King of England?

ALAIS Henry—you can't ever let them out.

HENRY You've lost me. Let who out?

ALAIS Your sons. You've put them in the dungeon and you've got to keep them there forever.

94

HENRY Do I now?

ALAIS If they're free when you die, it's the dungeon or the nunnery for me. I don't care which—a cell's a cell —but, Henry, what about the child?

HENRY Don't bother me about the child. The damn thing isn't born yet.

ALAIS If they're free, they'll kill it. I'm the one who'll live to see that and I will not see our children murdered.

HENRY You don't make the ultimatums: I do.

ALAIS Not this time. Either you keep them down forever or you find yourself another widow. I don't want the job.

HENRY Do you know what you're asking me to do?

ALAIS You locked your Queen up.

HENRY But my boys—how can I?

ALAIS That's for you to face.

HENRY You have no children.

ALAIS And I never will.

HENRY But they're my sons.

ALAIS I hate your sons. I'm not the one who wants a new line. If you want it, that's the price.

HENRY You'll come to Rome if I say so. You'll marry me if I say so. The boys go free if I say so. My terms are the only terms. The difficulty is, you see, the difficulty is you're right. (*So weary*) Incredible, but I have children

95

who would murder children. Every time I've read *Medea*, I've thought: "No; the thing's absurd. Fish eat their young, and foxes: but not us." And yet she did it. I imagine she was mad; don't you? Yes, mad she must have been.

(*He moves to go*)

ALAIS   Henry—are you going down?

HENRY   Down? Yes.

ALAIS   To let them out or keep them in?

HENRY   Could you say, to a child of yours, "You've seen the sunlight for the last time?"

ALAIS   Can you do it, Henry?

HENRY   Well, I'd be a master bastard if I did.

ALAIS   I must know. Can you?

HENRY   I shall have to, shan't I?
(*He goes*)

Dim and blackout

*The wine cellar, early morning. It is a large, dark and
vaulted place; its walls and heavy door are offstage, lost in
shadow. Candles flicker in tall candlesticks. There are
great casks of wine and one small table in the cellar; nothing else.*

RICHARD, JOHN *and* GEOFFREY *are on stage as the lights
rise.* JOHN, *at a cask of wine, is on the verge of replacing
a bung with a spigot.* RICHARD, *holding two cups, stands by
him.* GEOFFREY *stands apart.*

JOHN   The trick is not to dribble when you bang the
bung. (*He bangs it and slips the spigot into place*)
Voilà. I had an alcoholic Latin tutor—cup (RICHARD
hands him a cup)—who taught me all he knew.

GEOFFREY   Which wasn't much.

JOHN   I know I might as well be drunk.

GEOFFREY   If I were you, I'd worry.

JOHN   You know me—cup (*He gives* RICHARD *the full one
and takes the empty*)—I'd just worry over all the wrong
things.

GEOFFREY   Don't you know what's going to happen?

97

JOHN No, and you don't either. You and your big cere-
bellum. (*Doing* GEOFFREY) "I'm what's left. Here,
Daddy; here I am." And here you are.

RICHARD But not for long.

GEOFFREY You think we're getting out?

RICHARD No; deeper in. The fortress at Vaudreuil has
dungeons down two hundred feet. That's where I'd keep
us.

GEOFFREY And if I were Father, I'm not sure I'd keep the
three of us at all. You don't take prisoners; no, you don't.
And with good reason. Dungeon doors can swing both
ways but caskets have no hinges.

JOHN I know you. You only want to frighten me.

GEOFFREY John, the condition of your trousers, be they
wet or dry, could not concern me less. I think I'm apt to
die today and I am sweating, John. I'm sweating cold.

JOHN We've got friends.

GEOFFREY Name one.

JOHN Someone's got to rescue us.

GEOFFREY I can't think who or how or why.

RICHARD He isn't going to see me beg. He'll get no satis-
faction out of me.

GEOFFREY Why, you chivalric fool—as if the way one fell
down mattered.

RICHARD When the fall is all there is, it matters.

JOHN Can't we run or hide or anything?

RICHARD   Just in the wine.

JOHN (*Frightened by sounds of the cellar door opening*)
Geoff—
       (ELEANOR *appears. She carries a large covered
       breakfast tray. Like Henry, she hasn't slept*)

ELEANOR   My barge is leaving at eleven and I've come to
say good-bye.

GEOFFREY   Does Henry know you're here?

ELEANOR   The Queen still has some privileges. I bring
you breakfast.

JOHN   I'm not hungry.

GEOFFREY   What's he planning?

RICHARD   Is he going to keep us here?

ELEANOR   First, have a little nourishment.

RICHARD   For God's sake, Mother—

ELEANOR   Eat.
       (*She drops the tray on the table. It makes a great
       metallic clatter.* RICHARD *removes the cover. The
       tray contains a stack of daggers and short swords*)

GEOFFREY   Well, Eleanor.

RICHARD   How heavy is the outside guard?

ELEANOR   There's just the turnkey.

RICHARD   What about the courtyard and the gates?

ELEANOR   They're putting Henry's train together and it's
chaos. You can walk right out.

RICHARD We'll go to Poitiers. He'll expect that but we'll meet him with an army when he comes. (*To* GEOFFREY *and* JOHN) Keep close to me and when you run, run hard.

GEOFFREY Why run at all? I think we ought to stay.

JOHN Stay here?

GEOFFREY Till Henry comes. (*To* ELEANOR) He will come, won't he—and he'll come alone. (*To* RICHARD) I count three knives to one.

RICHARD You think we could?

JOHN I'd only do it wrong. You kill him and I'll watch.

GEOFFREY The three of us together: we must all three do it. I want us all responsible.

ELEANOR Don't listen to him. Take the knives and run.

GEOFFREY And miss this opportunity?

ELEANOR Get out.

GEOFFREY (*To* RICHARD) I'll be behind the door with John. You'll want to do it from the front. (*To* ELEANOR) And you, you lucky girl, you get to see the pageant.

ELEANOR Mother's looking for a name for you—if English has one adequately foul.

GEOFFREY Now hold on. I've been vilified enough. I've had enough of it. You brought the cutlery, you hauled it down here. Don't you dare tell me this wasn't in your mind.

ELEANOR I tell you. I deny it.

GEOFFREY   Swear on something. I'm agog to hear what you consider holy.
    (*She turns abruptly and starts to go*)

RICHARD   Where are you going?

ELEANOR   Up for air.

GEOFFREY   (*To* RICHARD, *who moves to intercept her*) Don't stop her.

RICHARD   But she'll warn him.

GEOFFREY   Let her go. She isn't going to tell him anything.

ELEANOR   You think I'm going to let this happen?

GEOFFREY   Frankly, Mother, your position on the board is poorish. If you tattled, there would be a rash of executions and you don't want that. No, you don't want to lose a one of us: not even me.

ELEANOR   You're clever but I wonder if you're right.

GEOFFREY   Oh, lady, don't you know where you are? You're in stalemate. Warn him, it's the end of us: warn him not and it's the end of him. It's that clear.

ELEANOR   (*Not very loud*) Guard.

GEOFFREY   Go on, dear. Call again—and pitch it up a little.

ELEANOR   I'll have him take the knives away.

RICHARD   And be the one to put us in Vaudreuil, down two hundred feet?

ELEANOR   Then run away; escape. You've still got time.

RICHARD No. Geoffrey's right; we'll stay.

ELEANOR You, too? Oh, Richard.

RICHARD Oh, oh, oh. There's nothing in your oh's: they're empty.

ELEANOR You're not an assassin.

RICHARD Look again.

ELEANOR You're not. You're my Richard and you love me.

RICHARD Let me kiss the nasty scratch and make it well.

ELEANOR Yes, do. Come let me hold you.

RICHARD You're more beautiful than ever. There is much that's beautiful in evil when it's absolutely pure. You are so foul you're fair. You stand there looking like a saint in pain when you brought us the knives to do your work.

ELEANOR That's not true.

RICHARD You did bring these things.

ELEANOR Not for this.

RICHARD Here—you want him dead, you do it.

ELEANOR You unnatural animal.

RICHARD Unnatural, Mummy? You tell me, what's nature's way? If poisoned mushrooms grow and babies come with crooked backs, if goiters thrive and dogs go mad and wives kill husbands, what's unnatural? Here stands your lamb. Come cover him with kisses; he's all yours.

ELEANOR No, you're not mine. I'm not responsible.

RICHARD Where do you think I learned this from? Who do you think I studied under? How old was I when you fought with Henry first?

ELEANOR Young . . . I don't know.

RICHARD How many battles did I watch?

ELEANOR But those were battles, not a knife behind a door.

RICHARD I've never heard a corpse ask how it got so cold. You've got a mind: you tell me, what was on it when you had your soldiers point their crossbows at him?

ELEANOR That was in the field.

RICHARD I don't care if it's in the dahlia bed. What were you thinking, Eleanor?

ELEANOR Of you.

RICHARD Of your unnatural animal?

ELEANOR I did it all for you.

RICHARD You wanted Father dead.

ELEANOR No, never that.

RICHARD You tried to kill him, didn't you?

ELEANOR Yes.

RICHARD Why? What did you want?

ELEANOR I wanted Henry back.

RICHARD You lie.

ELEANOR I wanted Henry. Isn't there a chair?

JOHN (*Handing her his cup of wine*) Here. (*She takes it and reaches out to touch his cheek. He draws away*) None of that.

ELEANOR I've done without it this long; I'll endure.

GEOFFREY She'll warn him. I was wrong. She'll do it if she gets the chance.

ELEANOR Then you're in stalemate, aren't you, lamb?

GEOFFREY How so?

ELEANOR You don't dare let me stay here and you don't dare let me out. Dear me, whatever shall we do with Mother?

GEOFFREY Offhand there are several possibilities.

JOHN (*There are sounds of the door opening as he races to the table and slams the cover on the tray*) Watch it. (HENRY *appears, carrying an armful of huge candles.* ALAIS *follows*)

HENRY (*As he fills the empty candlesticks and* ALAIS, *with a taper, lights them*) It wants light. What we do in dungeons needs the shades of day. I stole the candles from the chapel. No one minded. Jesus won't begrudge them and the chaplain works for me.

ELEANOR You look dreadful.

HENRY So do you.

ELEANOR I underslept a little.

104

HENRY We can all rest in a little while. (*The candles are lit. The room is warm and cheery*) That's better. Bright and clear, just like the morning.

ELEANOR Here: I'll take the breakfast things.

RICHARD Not yet.

ELEANOR They've gotten cold.

RICHARD They're good cold.

HENRY Listen to me. What's the answer? Can I ever let you out?

RICHARD What do you want from us? You must be mad. Why did you have to come here? Damn you, why'd you come?

HENRY You think I want to lock you up?

RICHARD You've got to. You can't let me out. You know you can't. I'll never stop.

HENRY I can't stop either.

RICHARD There's only fighting left.

HENRY Not even that. What have you got to fight me with?

ELEANOR (*As* RICHARD *and* GEOFFREY *start for the tray*) My children. In the past, I've come and gone and loved you when it suited me. I never nursed you, warmed you, washed you, fed you, but today I felt such love for each of you and so I brought you breakfast.

RICHARD Mother.

HENRY Let her be.

ELEANOR (*Removing the cover*) I thought I had no other choice but I was wrong again.

HENRY Brave boys; that's what I have. Three warriors. Who had first crack? How was I divided up? Christ—

RICHARD You drove us to it.

HENRY Don't stop now. You're killers, aren't you? I am. I can do it. (*To* GEOFFREY) Take a knife. (*To* RICHARD) Come on. What is it? Come for me.

RICHARD I can't.

HENRY You're Richard, aren't you?

RICHARD But you're Henry.

HENRY Please. We can't stop and we can't go back. There's nothing else.

JOHN Daddy? Take me back. Please. Can't we try again?

HENRY Again?

JOHN We always have before.

HENRY Oh yes . . . we always have.

JOHN (*Running toward him, arms outstretched*) Oh, Daddy—
    (*He comes skidding to a stop as* HENRY *draws his sword and holds it leveled at* JOHN's *vitals*)

ELEANOR Go on. Execute them. You're the King. You've judged. You've sentenced. You know how.

HENRY By God, I will. Come Monday and they'll hang you with the washing. There'll be princes swinging from the Christmas trees.

ELEANOR Why wait? They are assassins, aren't they? This was treason, wasn't it? You gave them life—you take it.

HENRY Who's to say it's monstrous? I'm the King. I call it just. (*To his sons*) Therefore, I, Henry, by the Grace of God King of the English, Lord of Scotland, Ireland and Wales, Count of Anjou, Brittany, Poitou and Normandy, Maine, Gascony and Aquitaine, do sentence you to death. Done this Christmas Day in Chinon in God's year eleven eighty-three. (*He moves to* RICHARD, *sword raised. He swings the sword through the air and brings it crashing to the cellar floor. Into the silence he speaks, softly and thoughtfully*) Surely that's not what I intended. Children . . . Children are . . . They're all we have. (*Spent, shattered, unable to look at anyone or anything, he waves them from the room*) Go on. I'm done, I'm done. I'm finished with you. Never come again.

(JOHN, GEOFFREY *and* RICHARD *exit*)

ELEANOR You spare the rod, you'll spoil those boys.

HENRY I couldn't do it, Eleanor.

ELEANOR Nobody thought you could.

HENRY I did.

ALAIS You saved them. You maneuvered it.

ELEANOR Did I?

ALAIS They're free because of you. They'll kill him one day; you know that.

ELEANOR The next time or the next.

ALAIS You always win, *Maman.*

ELEANOR Except the prize.

ALAIS (*To* HENRY) Come rest.

HENRY I want no women in my life.

ALAIS You're tired.

HENRY I could have conquered Europe, all of it, but I had women in my life.

ALAIS I'll warm some wine.

HENRY I've shot your world, you silly bitch, and there you stand, all honey and molasses. Sweet? You make my teeth ache.
(*They embrace*)

ELEANOR That's touching. Is it for my benefit?

HENRY Your benefit? (*To* ALAIS) Get out. Go on. Go.

ALAIS When you want me, I'll be waiting.
(*She exits*)

HENRY (*Turning on* ELEANOR) For your benefit? I've done enough on your account. I should have killed you years ago.

ELEANOR There's no one peeking. Do it now.

HENRY I've wasted fortunes, squandered lives, spent everything—to buy this pit. I've got an eye for value. This is what I've made. I meant to do so much.

ELEANOR Is this a play for pity?

HENRY Not from you. You put me here. You made me do mad things. You've bled me.

ELEANOR Shoulder it yourself. Don't put it on my back.

You've done what you have done and no one but yourself has made you do it. Pick it up and carry it. I can.
My losses are my work.

HENRY What losses? I've been cheated, not you. I'm the
one with nothing.

ELEANOR Lost your life's work, have you? Provinces are
nothing: land is dirt. I've lost you. I can't ever have
you back again. You haven't suffered. I could take defeats like yours and laugh. I've done it. If you're broken,
it's because you're brittle. You are all that I have ever
loved. Christ, you don't know what nothing is. I want
to die.

HENRY You don't.

ELEANOR I want to die.

HENRY I'll hold you.

ELEANOR I want to die.

HENRY Stop saying that. Let me do something, damn
you. This is terrible.

ELEANOR Henry, I want to die.

HENRY You will, you know. Wait long enough and it'll
happen.

ELEANOR (*Smiling*) So it will.

HENRY We're in the cellar and you're going back to prison
and my life is wasted and we've lost each other and
you're smiling.

ELEANOR It's the way I register despair. There's everything in life but hope.

HENRY   We have each other and for all I know that's what
hope is.

ELEANOR   We're jungle creatures, Henry, and the dark is
all around us. See them? In the corners, you can see the
eyes.

HENRY   And they can see ours. I'm a match for anything.
Aren't you?

ELEANOR   I should have been a great fool not to love you.

HENRY   Come along; I'll see you to your ship.

ELEANOR   So soon?

HENRY   There's always Easter Court.

ELEANOR   You'll let me out for Easter?

HENRY   Come the resurrection, you can strike me down
again.

ELEANOR   Perhaps I'll do it next time.

HENRY   And perhaps you won't.

ELEANOR   (*Taking his arm, moving to go*)   It must be late
and I don't want to miss the tide.

HENRY   (*As they go*)   You know, I hope we never die.

ELEANOR   I hope so, too.

HENRY   You think there's any chance of it?

Curtain